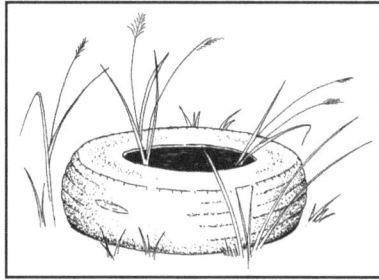

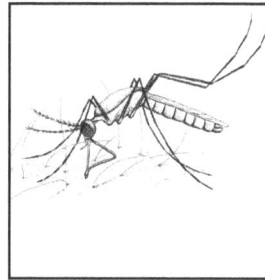

The Mosquito Book

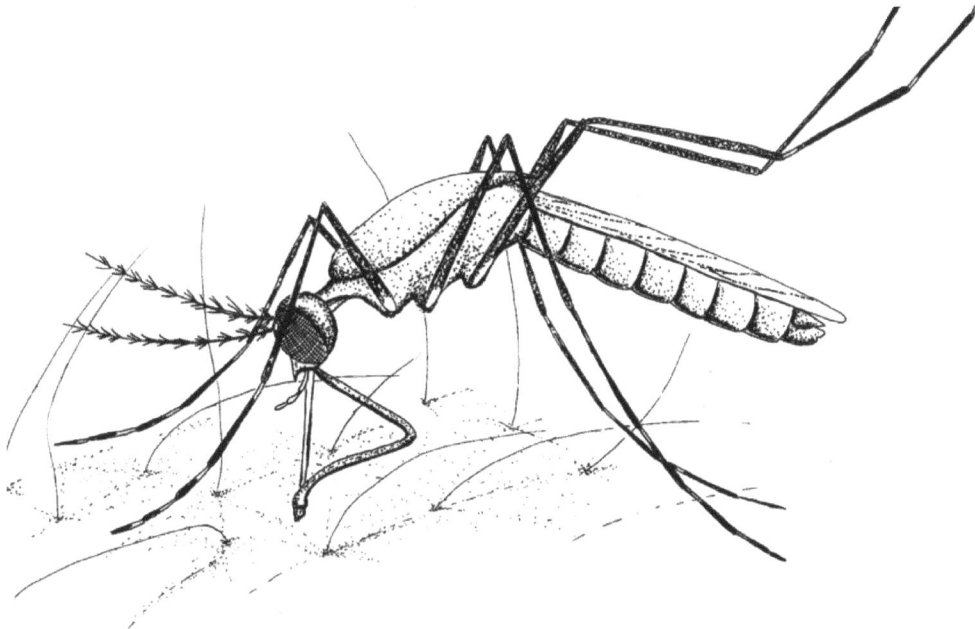

I0118531

Footprint: A Belizean Environmental Series

The Mosquito Book is the second in this series aimed at enlightening Belizeans about the issues affecting their health and environment.

Books in this series:

The Mosquito Book

Ed Boles
Aquatic Ecologist

Footprint: A Belizean Environmental Series 2

Copyright © 2016 Ed Boles
Published by *Producciones de la Hamaca*, Caye Caulker, Belize
<producciones-hamaca.com>

ISBN: 978-976-8142-93-1 (print edition)
ISBN: 978-976-8142-94-8 (e-book edition)
The Mosquito Book is the second in the series, *Footprint: A Belizean Environmental Series*
ISBN: 978-976-8142-788

Illustrations Copyright © 2016 Ed Boles

This book was printed on-demand by Lightning Source, Inc (LSI). The on-demand printing system is environmentally friendly because books are printed as needed, instead of in large numbers that might end up in someone's basement or a dump site. In addition, LSI is committed to using materials obtained by sustainable forestry practices. LSI is certified by Sustainable Forestry Initiative (SFI® Certificate Number: PwC-SFICOC-345 SFI-00980). The Sustainable Forestry Initiative (SFI) is an independent, internationally recognized non-profit organization responsible for the SFI certification standard, the world's largest single forest certification standard. The SFI program is based on the premise that responsible environmental behavior and sound business decisions can co-exist to the benefit of communities, customers and the environment, today and for future generations <sfiprogram.org>.

Producciones de la Hamaca is dedicated to:
—Celebration and documentation of Earth and all her inhabitants,
—Restoration and conservation of Earth's natural resources,
—Creative expression of the sacredness of Earth and Spirit.

Contents

Preface

Years ago, as a medical entomologist working in the United States, I realized the close relationship we share with mosquitoes, their importance as pest and disease vectors, and the amount of pesticides we spray in cities, towns, and villages to control their population numbers. It was also evident that most of our urban mosquito problems are created by all of us as we unintentionally build mosquito breeding habitats around our yards and neighbourhoods, schools, parks, and drainage ditches. If we are a major part of the problem, we can also be a solution to the problem. What we need is an awareness and understanding of the real causes behind increases in mosquito populations, and knowledge about various non-chemical, low-cost control strategies that can be put into place through community involvement.

With that in mind, the predecessor to *The Mosquito Book* was written as an activities manual designed to be used to supplement junior high school and high school science classes. It was also intended to be an activity manual encouraging development of neighbourhood mosquito survey and non-chemical control programmes. This manual has been re-drafted and updated into a booklet to supplement science studies within Belize, and to encourage the spread of awareness and the idea that communities can and must play a vital role in controlling mosquito breeding issues within our neighbourhoods.

The Mosquito Book focuses on some of the important mosquito disease vectors found in Belize. It also includes those old diseases have been around for generations, as well as newer diseases, and a new mosquito species, that has arrived in Belize very recently. This book is offered as a supplementary text for 1st through 4th Form science classes and as a community awareness reference. The technical terms used throughout the text are in bold where they are first used, and each term is also defined in the glossary at the end. It is my hope that this will be a useful book for helping us better understand our intimate connections with mosquitoes, the roles we as community members can play in helping reduce their numbers, and therefore the diseases they carry, without spraying ourselves with pesticides and destroying the natural habitats where some mosquito species live.

Ed Boles

April, 2016

Introduction

Have you ever been awakened by the hum of a hungry mosquito? How did it get into your bedroom? Perhaps it came in through an open door or a tiny hole in your window screen. But where did this mosquito come from? Chances are they are breeding right in your own backyard. Mosquitoes are such small, fragile insects. Yet they can have a major effect on our lives. They can quickly take the fun out of an afternoon football game. They can discourage fishing and camping trips. They can drive tourists away from resort areas and bring outdoor work to a halt. They pester our pets and livestock.

We humans share the world with millions of other species. However, few other creatures have as intimate a relationship with us as do mosquitoes. Several species of these fragile, scaly-winged flies have been constant companions of humans throughout our history. We have carried mosquitoes around the world. We make comfortable breeding sites for them to grow wherever we live and provide females with blood meals for making eggs.

Occasionally mosquitoes repay us by serving as vectors for such diseases as **malaria**, **yellow fever**, **dengue fever**, **chikungunya**, and the most recently introduced disease to Belize—**Zika**. Epidemics of mosquito-borne diseases have occurred often and in many places in the world, and have had a strong influence on our species. Usually such outbreaks are directly or indirectly connected to negative influences we humans impose on our environments that increase mosquito breeding sites and, consequently, mosquito numbers.

Our garbage piles, discarded tires, and anything else that holds water provides ample breeding sites for mosquitoes. In particular, the yellow fever mosquito, and its close cousin that has recently arrived in Belize, the Asian tiger mosquito, prefer these water-holding containers that we provide them. Sewage-tainted ditches are excellent habitats for southern house mosquitoes. Dams and other flow obstructions in rivers and streams encourage many kinds of mosquitoes, including malaria-transmitting mosquitoes. Rearing of cattle and other livestock in marsh areas is a good way to provide both habitat (every water-filled foot print) and a ready blood meal, guaranteeing an increase in marsh mosquito numbers.

Mosquito-Borne Diseases

Mosquitoes are far more than just pests! They are vectors for infectious agents (viruses, bacteria, protozoa, nematodes) that have caused disease epidemics in humans and our domestic animals throughout time. Millions of people around the world become sick with these diseases each year. Hundreds of thousands die. Thus, mosquitoes have also had a major impact on local and regional history.

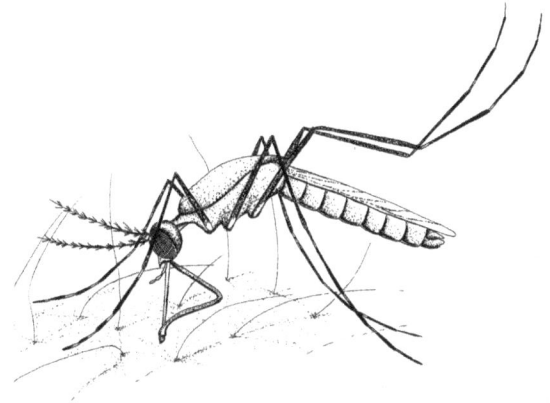

The link between human sickness and certain kinds of insects has been suspected for centuries. The role of insects as disease carriers was not proven until the last half of the nineteenth century. In 1877, Patrick Manson found that Bancroftian filarial worms (*Wuchereria bancrofti*) passed through a developmental stage in a *Culex* mosquito. This discovery marked the birth of medical entomology as a major field of study.

Vectors can carry diseases in two ways. Houseflies and roaches walk across garbage, human waste, or infectious wounds. They can pick up certain kinds of bacteria, viruses, protozoans and worm eggs on their legs and feet. Should these vectors enter our homes and contaminate our food, they will transmit these pathogens and parasites to us. These insects are called **mechanical vectors** because they are just physical transporters of infectious agents.

Other kinds of parasites and pathogens use their vectors as hosts, passing through developmental stages within these **biological vectors**. Only then can the infectious agents successfully enter the next host, the one chosen by the vector for a blood meal. Mosquitoes, black flies, and ticks fall into this important group of vectors. Mosquitoes found in Belize and the diseases they carry are listed in Table 1, although not all of these diseases have been confirmed within the country.

Table 1
Mosquito-borne Infectious Agents Carried by
Mosquitoes Found within Belize and the Region

Disease (*Infectious Agent*)	Human Symptoms	Mosquito Vector	Reservoir
eastern equine encephalitis (*Alphavirus* genus)	fever, headache	some *Aedes*, *Coquillettidia* and *Culex*	possibly birds, rodents, bats, reptiles, amphibians, mosquito eggs, sometimes adult mosquitoes
Venezuelan equine encephalitis (*Alphavirus* genus)	fever, headache	include *Aedes, Psorophora, Masnonia,* and *Deinocerites, with Aedes aegypti* being the primary human vector	
western equine encephalitis (*Alphavirus* genus)	fever, headache	some *Culex*	
St. Louis encephalitis (*Flavivirus* genus)	fever, headache	some *Culex*	
dengue fever types 1,2,3,4 (*Flavavirus* genus)	fever, rash, bone pain bleeding (haemorhagic form)	*Aedes aegypti, Aedes albopictus*	humans, mosquitoes
yellow fever (*Flavavirus* genus)	fever, headache, backache, nausea	*Aedes aegypti, Aedes albopictus*	humans, mosquitoes
chikungunya (*Alphavirus* genus)	Fever, headache, nausea	*Aedes aegypti*	unknown
Zika (*Flavavirus* genus)	fever, joint pain, rash, conjunctivitis (red eyes), possible birth defects (microcephaly and other abnormalities) if pregnant women are infected	*Aedes aegypti*	humans, mosquitoes
malaria (*Plasmodium vivax, P. falciparum*)	Fever, chills, sweats, headache, shock, renal and liver failure, coma	*Anopheles*	humans
blood fluke (*Wuchereria bancrofti*)	Filarial fever, lymphangitis, elephantiasis	*Culex quinquefaciatus, Anopheles, Aedes*	humans
dog heartwarm (*Dirofilaria immitis*)	Chest pain, cough, fibrotic nodes	several species of *Culex*	domestic dogs

Malaria is one of the most widespread and life threatening diseases in the world. It is a very ancient disease that has probably been around at least since the beginning of humans. There are also many other forms of malaria that infect other animals. Female *Anopheles* mosquitoes carry malaria from infected people to healthy people. The sexual stage of the malaria parasite, a protozoan in the genus *Plasmodium*, is taken up by the mosquito with the blood as it feeds from an infected person. Once inside of the mosquito's stomach, *Plasmodium* cells unite and form cysts in the stomach wall. Within eight days to a month, each cyst releases thousands of **sporozoites**, some of which migrate to the mosquito's salivary glands. When the sickly female mosquito (she has malaria too!) bites the next human, these infective sporozoites enter the new host's blood stream, who may then suffer from malaria as the *Plasmodium* cells continue their life cycle. Malaria incidence in Belize peaked in 1994 with nearly 10,000 cases. By the year 2000 the incidence was down to under 1500 and in 2010 there were only 156 cases of malaria in Belize.

Yellow fever mosquitoes (*Aedes aegypti*) and Asian tiger mosquitoes (*Aedes albopictus*) breed in containers around our homes. These mosquitoes can carry viruses that cause yellow fever, dengue fever, chikungunya, and Zika. Yellow fever epidemics have claimed many lives. Usually monkey populations harbour the yellow fever virus. During the mid-1950s, a great many howler monkeys and spider monkeys in Belize died due to a yellow fever epidemic, which completely eliminated those monkey species in some areas of Belize. When mosquitoes that feed on infected monkeys bite humans, the disease can be rapidly spread through rural villages. Humans infected with the virus carry yellow fever to the cities, where they are bitten by urban mosquitoes that can potentially spread the disease to thousands. In 2016 travel advisories state that there is no risk of yellow fever infection in Belize.

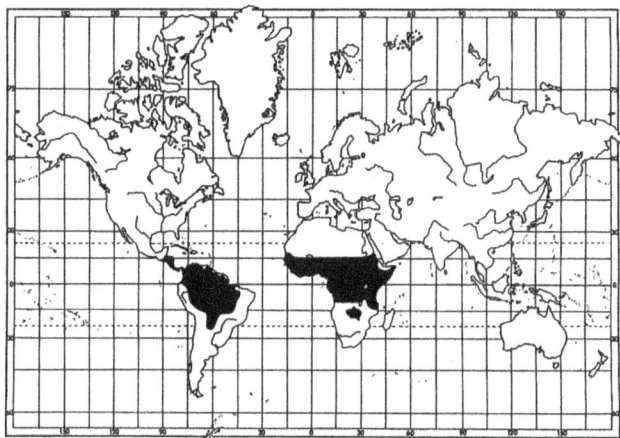

Areas of the World Where Malaria Occurs

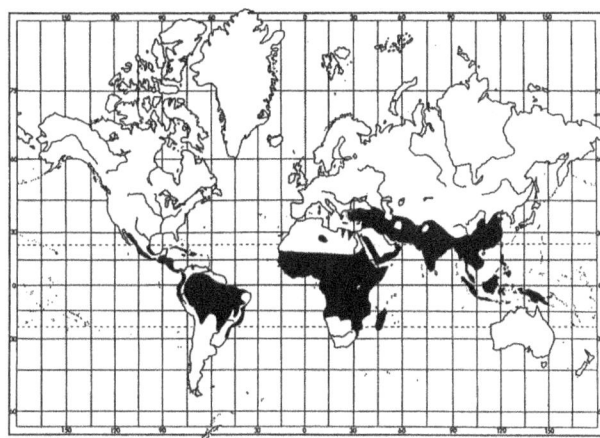

Areas of the World Where Yellow Fever Occurs

Dengue fever is generally not fatal, but people become very sick. **Dengue haemorrhagic fever** can develop, which is fatal in many cases. When a dengue fever epidemic occurred in Texas and Louisiana in 1922, from one to two million people were affected. During 1972, 1.5 million people suffered from dengue fever in Columbia. The largest outbreak of dengue fever in the Americas lasted from 1977 to 1980. Cases were reported from northern South America to Texas. Belize government health authorities warned of an increasing incidence of dengue fever in 2015 with over 250 cases by August.

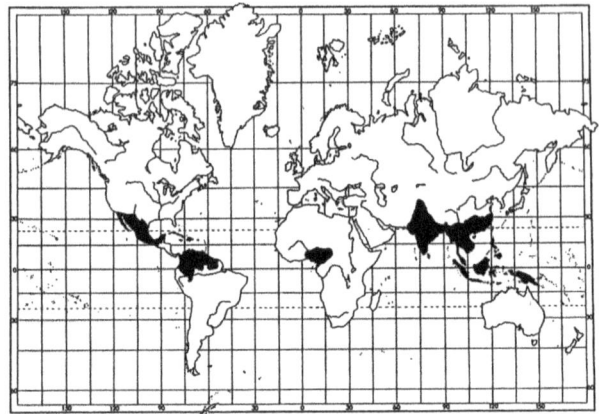

Areas of the World Where Dengue Fever Occurs

Another disease called chikungunya, very similar to dengue fever, has invaded the Americas. The first case of chikungunya in the Western Hemisphere was reported from Saint Martin in 2013. By 2014 chikungunya had been reported in 31 countries and territories throughout the region. Several cases have been reported in Belize.

Zika virus, transmitted by *Aedes aegypti* and certain other *Aedes* species, is the newest disease to arrive in our region. It was first found in 1947 in monkeys from Uganda, and the first human infection was diagnosed in 1954 in Nigeria. Then outbreaks occurred in other areas of Africa, southeast Asia, and the Pacific islands. Zika is thought to have been introduced to Brazil in 2013. Since the first case of Zika was reported in Brazil in May 2015, the virus has rapidly spread throughout the Americas. Belize had no cases reported until May 2016 and the U.S. Center for Disease Control has issued a travel warning for the country. Symptoms caused by Zika are similar to dengue fever, but much milder. However, studies have linked the disease to **microcephaly**, a birth defect in which babies are born with very small heads and under-developed brains, when pregnant women are infected with the disease. Zika virus has also been shown to be transmitted sexually. Vaccines against Zika virus show promising early results in monkeys.

Mosquitoes can carry many other kinds of viruses causing diseases. The St. Louis Encephalitis virus (SLE) builds up in bird flocks. Southern house mosquitoes (*Culex quinquefaciatus)* feed on both birds and humans and can carry this virus from infected birds to people. SLE is in most areas of the world where yellow fever and dengue fever occurs, including Central America and the Caribbean. Other types of **encephalitis viruses** carried by mosquitoes affect horses as well as humans (eastern equine encephalitis, western equine encephalitis). These viral infections can cause high fever and swelling of parts of the brain and spinal cord. Permanent brain damage can occur. These diseases are particularly severe on young children and elderly people.

Some mosquitoes can carry nematode parasites that affect humans. Over 250 million people are infected with nematodes that cause **Bancroftian** and **Brugian filariasis**. The adult **round worms** live in the victim's **lymph system**. There they block the flow of lymph fluids. Low infections can cause little problem. Heavy infections, however, can lead to extreme swelling of arms and legs, becoming particularly evident in the elderly. This condition is called "**elephantiasis**".

Dog heartworms are carried by many different species of mosquitoes. Adult worms live in the dog's heart, where heavy infections disrupt function and shorten the dog's life. Infections in humans cause lung damage.

Many mosquito-borne diseases have been eliminated, or at least reduced, in many parts of the world. However, the mosquitoes that can carry these disease agents are still present. Sometimes these diseases return to areas where they had been eradicated, being re-introduced by travellers, immigrants, and military personnel coming from countries where these diseases are still active. Some of these people carry the disease pathogens or parasites in their blood, and a few may be bitten by mosquitoes that can transmit the disease to other people. Most of these diseases can only be controlled by controlling the mosquito populations that carry them.

Many human activities increase mosquito-breeding habitats, increasing the potential spread of mosquito-borne diseases. Damming rivers to control flooding or to create electricity has increased malaria in many places. Irrigation of crops such as rice has resulted in extensive mosquito problems. Almost everything we buy is packaged in containers that are thrown away after use. Many of these jars, cans, bottles, plastic wrappers, along with old washing machines and worn out tires, will hold water and breed mosquitoes. Such breeding sites are collectively referred to as "**artificial containers**". Increasing numbers of people traveling around the world and increasing international trade have helped to spread mosquito species and the diseases they carry into areas where they did not occur before.

Often our answer to solving mosquito problems, created both by nature and our own environmentally irresponsible behaviours, has been to douse our neighbourhoods with pesticides on a routine basis. Modern mosquito control agencies now use alternative approaches, efforts that rely on an understanding of mosquito **ecology**, population monitoring and use of non-chemical solutions such as environmental education, neighbourhood clean-up campaigns, and biological control. Usually those mosquito control solutions are long-term and ecologically sensitive, but also good for the health of our environment and the many other species that share it with us.

Over 50,000 tons of pesticides are used worldwide each year to battle mosquitoes. At least eighty-nine species of mosquitoes have developed resistance to different types of pesticides. If used incorrectly, these chemicals kill beneficial insects and wildlife. Many swamps and marshes have been drained to control mosquito breeding. Such actions result in severe ecological losses to local and regional communities. These wetlands are important nurseries for oysters, clams, shrimp, crabs and fish that supply commercial fisheries, provide habitat for many species of wildlife, absorb flood waters, and help to recharge our aquifers.

In contrast, **biological controls**, such as, **pathogens**, **parasites** and **predators** are being used to fight mosquitoes. Mosquito fish (*Gambusia affinis*) have been used all round the world as mosquito control agents since the 1940s. Special strains of bacteria kill mosquito larvae without harming other important animals. Scientists are testing other kinds of bacteria, viruses, **fungi**, protozoans, **planarians,** nematodes, copepods, fishes and even plants as mosquito control agents. In the near future, perhaps other biological mosquito control agents will be discovered.

Many cities, towns, and villages have mosquito control programmes. Some programmes rely almost exclusively on pesticides as the primary control strategy. The best programmes practice **integrated mosquito control,** including mosquito population monitoring, community education programmes, reduction of breeding sites, controlling mosquito larvae (**larviciding**) and attacking adults (**adulticiding**). Once artificial containers are eliminated, reducing breeding sites, biological control agents can be used to control mosquito larvae breeding in places that cannot be removed. Finally, chemicals are used only when all other efforts have failed or in times of emergencies (floods, hurricanes).

To control mosquitoes effectively, technicians have to know what species of mosquitoes are problems. This allows technicians and managers to understand more about the biology and ecology of problem mosquito species. Different mosquito species have different behaviours, require both different and overlapping habitats, and require different control strategies. This knowledge helps to prescribe and maintain effective control measures for those species of concern, particularly when mosquito populations are routinely monitored to evaluate control effectiveness.

Mosquito control programmes cannot do the job alone. They need our help. They need the involvement of our communities to get rid of breeding sites around homes. Community support can reduce mosquito numbers and reduce the amount of pesticides that must be used. Together we can reduce the chance of disease outbreaks and reduce our exposure to pesticides. Find out how you can support your local mosquito control programme.

Mosquito Growth and Development

A lot of people are not aware that a mosquito's life begins in water. They do not need very much water either. An old fruit jar tossed in the weeds will collect an inch or two of rainwater. The mosquito that stole a drop of your blood in the night might find the jar. She will then lay her eggs there. If she is a southern house mosquito, she will deposit her eggs glued together into a tiny raft on the water's surface. The gray egg raft, smaller than a grain of rice, can be made of one hundred to three hundred eggs. If she is a yellow fever mosquito, eggs will be glued to the side of the jar just above the water. When it rains again, the water level in the jar will rise. The eggs will flood and hatch, many of them almost instantly.

Metamorphosis

Mosquitoes go through **metamorphosis** as they grow. Metamorphosis is a change in form. The tiny **larva** wiggles out of the egg and begins to feed, grow, molt, and grow some more. The larva will then change into a **pupa** before it emerges as an adult. This aquatic part of a mosquito's life cycle can last from a week or ten days to a couple of weeks, depending on the species and environmental factors, such as, temperature and food.

As they grow and pass through each stage of metamorphosis, the mosquito will **molt** or shed its skin. The shed skin is called an **exuvia**. Larvae will molt four times and then change into a non-feeding, but very mobile pupa. During this pupal stage, the larval mosquito is transformed into an adult mosquito. The emerging adult mosquito carefully climbs out of the pupal skin hanging from the water's surface when that skin splits open. Adult mosquitoes do not molt.

Mosquitoes, and all other flies, butterflies, moths and beetles, go through **complete metamorphosis**. This means that each stage of development looks different from other stages. Also, larvae use different kinds of food than used by adults. Larvae filter small bits of food from the water while adults feed on plant juices and some feed on blood. Pupae do not feed.

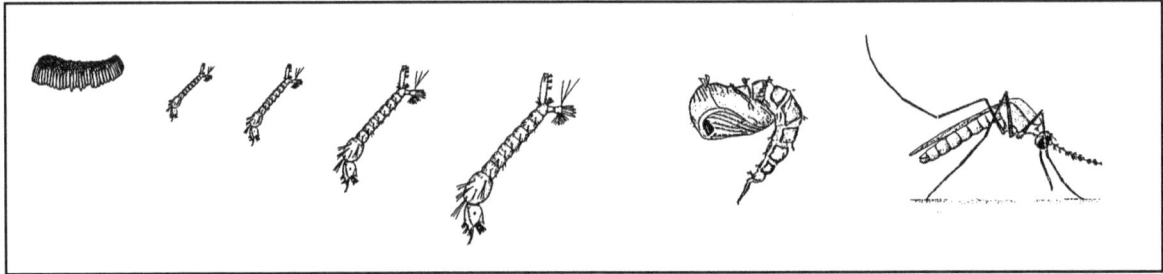

Complete Metamorphosis

Mosquitoes go from egg, through four larval instars (molting between each instar), and a pupa phase before becoming adults.

Other kinds of insects undergo **incomplete metamorphosis**. Each stage looks much like the last. There is no pupa or non-feeding stage. This is characteristic of those insect groups that first appeared on Earth. These are the more primitive insects. Cockroaches, grasshoppers and true bugs go through this kind of development.

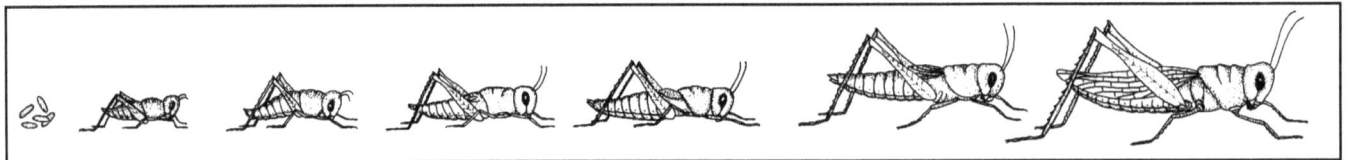

Incomplete Metamorphosis

More primitive insects go from egg, through several nymph stages (immature forms) and finally reaching the adult stage.

Mosquito eggs

Culex **egg rafts** can be found floating on the surface of still waters. The gravid female *Culex* mosquito will alight on the surface of a quiet body of water and begin depositing one egg after another, carefully sticking them together to create a tiny floating raft. Eggs are white when they are first laid, but soon turn to a dark gray colour. The eggs repel water molecules, which helps them stay afloat until the larvae hatch.

Other mosquitoes lay different kinds of eggs. Mosquitoes in the genus *Anopheles* lay single eggs on the water surface. Each egg has tiny floats on the sides. These expanded floats help to keep the water repellent *Anopheles* eggs on the surface until they hatch.

Some *Aedes* mosquitoes lay single eggs on damp ground, where they remain dry until rains fill these depressions. Other *Aedes* species stick their eggs to dry sides of water holding containers. *Aedes* eggs will hatch when containers become filled with rainwater. Several types of eggs are shown below.

Female mosquitoes of some species of *Aedes* look for a water-holding tree hole, coconut shell, or bromeliad in which to lay eggs. They attach their eggs to the inside wall of the tree hole or bromeliad above the water. Other species look for a shallow depression in the ground that may collect and hold water during and after a rain. *Aedes aegypti* specialize in using artificial containers, such as old tires, discarded washing machines, cans, jars, or any other object that holds water, also gluing their eggs above the water. In all of these cases the eggs stay dry as the embryos develop and rest until the next rain, when the waters rise and flood the eggs. Once water reaches the eggs, many of them will hatch almost instantly, larvae wiggling free to begin feeding and growing. Some of the eggs may remain unhatched until the next rains. Should no rains follow and the water dry up before the hatched larvae can develop into adults, the unhatched eggs are ready when the next rain does come.

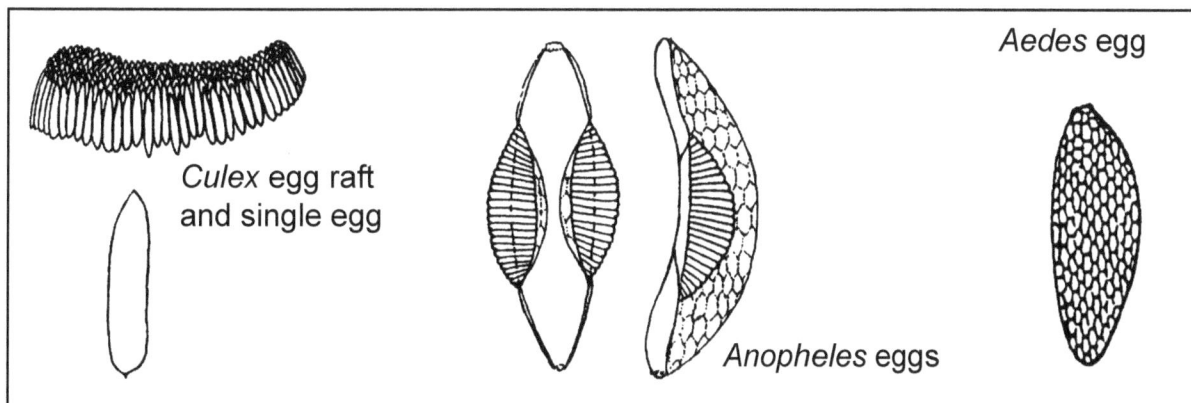

Aedes egg

Culex egg raft
and single egg

Anopheles eggs

Hatching Mosquitoes

Mosquitoes are easy to hatch and rear. Many people grow mosquitoes right in their own yards without really trying or knowing. A good way to learn about mosquitoes is to watch them up close as they hatch and go through their life cycle. Find a quiet pool of water, a stagnant ditch, or an old tire holding water and examine the surface of the water closely for egg rafts. Collect an egg raft by scooping it up with a small strip of paper. Fill a large glass jar, preferably one with smooth sides that has had the labels scrapped off, about half full of water from the same site where you collected the eggs. Gently place the egg raft on the surface of the water in the jar. Sprinkle a small pinch of baker's yeast in the water for the larva to feed on when they hatch. Place a small piece of window screen over the mouth of the jar and hold it in place with string, tape or rubber bands. Make sure that the screen is in place and that mosquitoes cannot escape the jar once they become adults. Sit the jar in a quiet place where it will not get direct sunlight. Observe the jar every day over a couple of weeks and note what happens.

Studying Larvae

The larva is a special stage in the mosquito's life cycle. This is the growing stage when the mosquito accumulates fat. Larvae are very active swimmers. They spend a lot of time feeding. Watch the swimming larvae wiggling as they move up and down in the water. Notice how they go to the bottom of the jar and graze on food particles that accumulate there. Notice how the larvae hang upside down from the surface and see their small mouth parts moving as they filter particles of food from the water. How do they attach themselves to the water's surface?

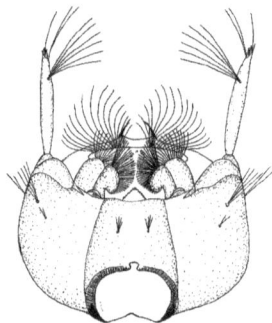

swimming larvae

mouth brushes of larva

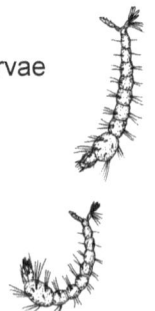

Parts of Mosquito Larvae

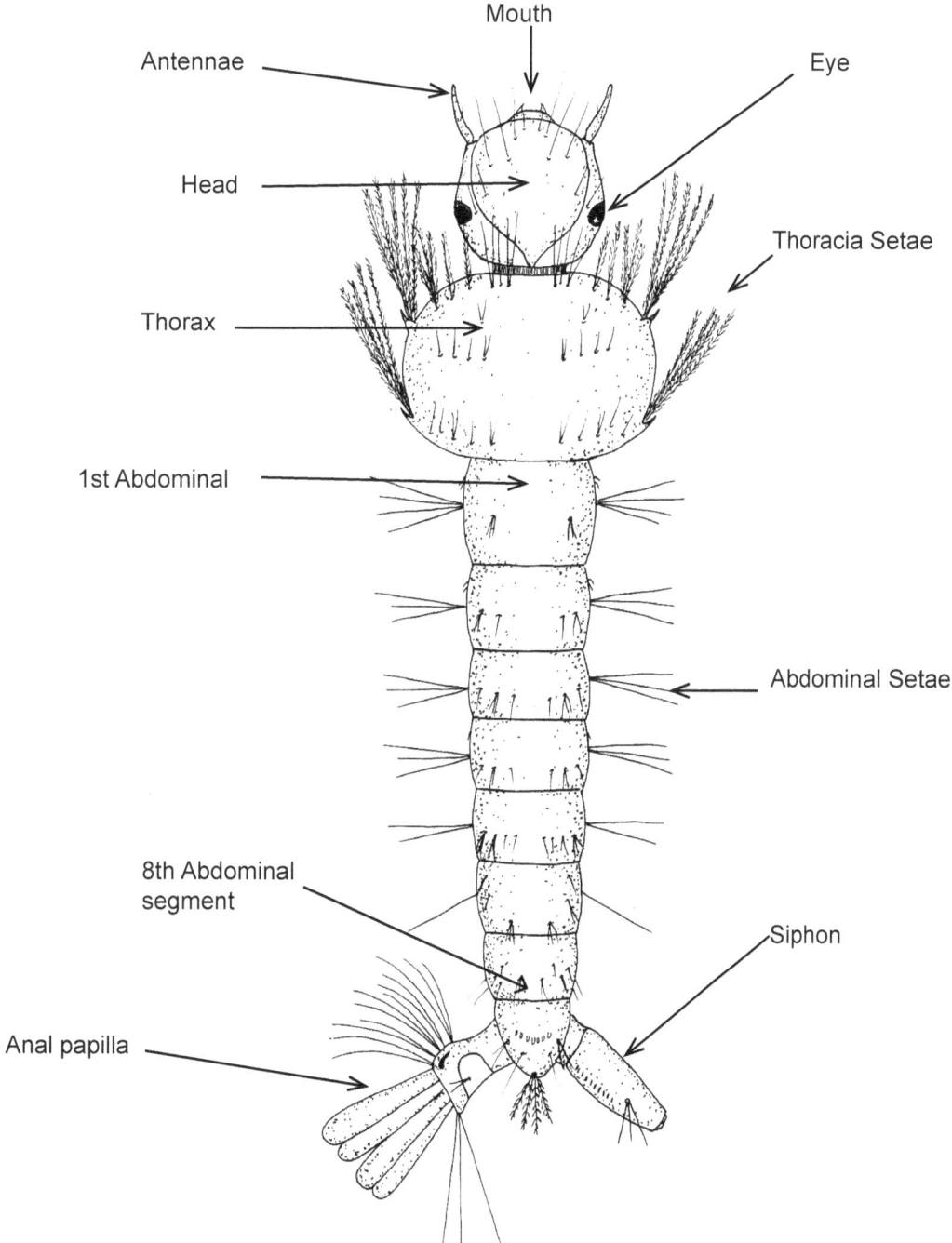

Mouth

Antennae

Eye

Head

Thoracia Setae

Thorax

1st Abdominal

Abdominal Setae

8th Abdominal segment

Siphon

Anal papilla

Studying Pupae

Pupae do not feed. Instead, they are busy going through a major change. At the end of the pupal stage, the mosquito will change from an aquatic to a terrestrial insect. The pupal stage of many insects is spent resting in a **cocoon** or case. The mosquito pupa, however, is still very active. Pupae will turn into adult mosquitoes within a few days' time. How do the pupae swim? Do they swim as much as the larvae? Their swimming motions have earned them the name **"tumblers"**. They have broad paddles on the tips of their abdomens.

Notice how pupae will swim to the bottom when the side of the jar is tapped or when a shadow passes over them. Why? The skin covering the head and thorax of the pupa holds a tiny pocket of air. This bubble helps the pupa stay at the surface.

Quiescent Pupa of a Moth

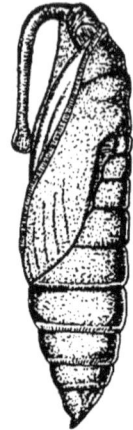

Parts of Mosquito Pupa

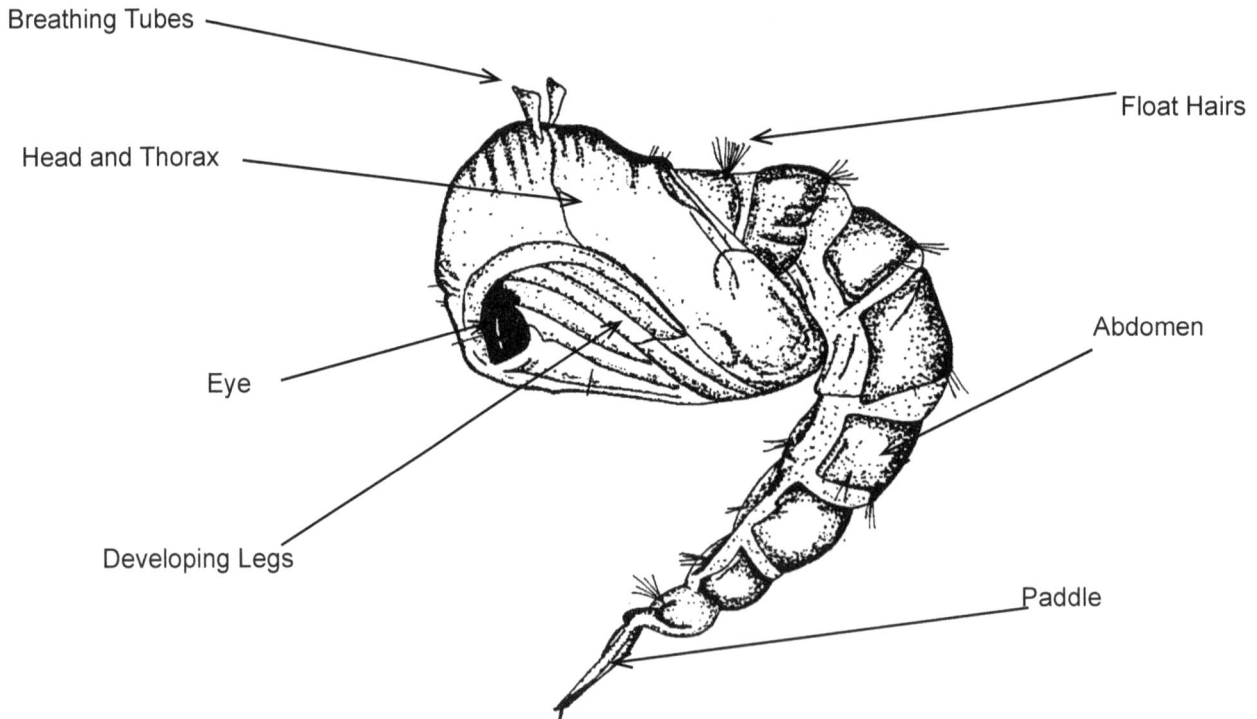

Breathing Tubes

Head and Thorax

Eye

Developing Legs

Float Hairs

Abdomen

Paddle

Studying Adult Mosquitoes

Adult mosquitoes feed on plant juices in the wild. They suck the juices through their proboscis. The **proboscis** is made up of seven different parts. The outer sleeve bends out of the way during feeding. Male adult mosquitoes feed only on plant juices while most adult female mosquitoes also use their mouth parts to penetrate the skin of their hosts, piercing into **capillaries** and sucking out blood.

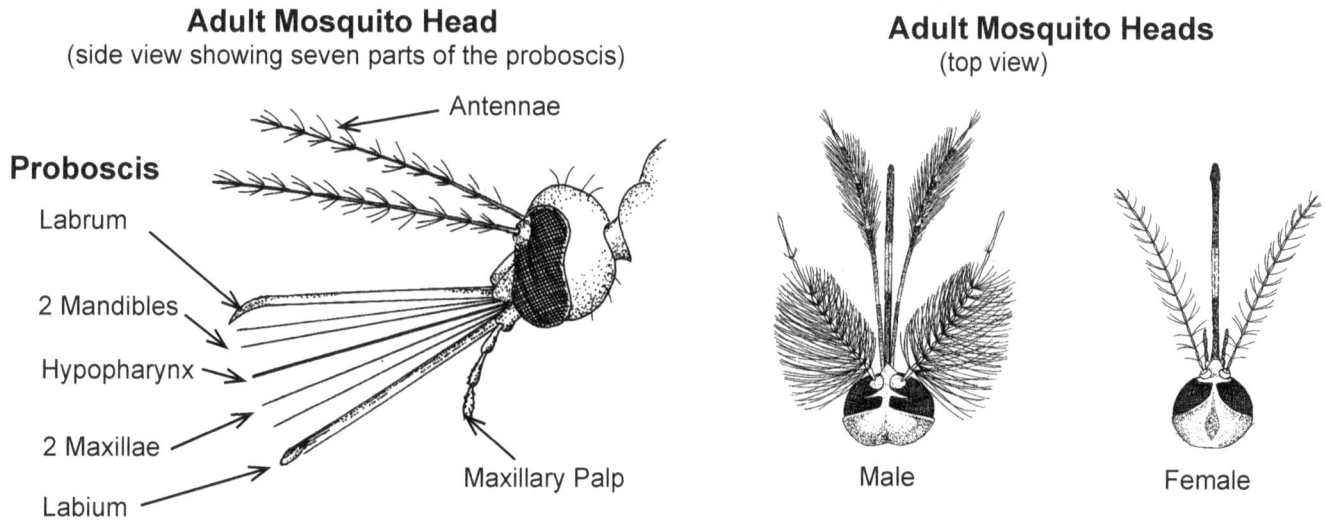

Adult Mosquito Head
(side view showing seven parts of the proboscis)

Adult Mosquito Heads
(top view)

Antennae

Proboscis

Labrum

2 Mandibles

Hypopharynx

2 Maxillae

Labium

Maxillary Palp

Male

Female

Why is it that only the female mosquito feeds on blood? Blood is high in protein and is important for the development of eggs. The female mosquito can detect **carbon dioxide** exhaled by a host. Depending on the species of mosquito, this host may be a dog or a cat; it might be a horse or a cow or a bird; or it could be a turtle or snake. Often that host is you or me. The female mosquito can follow this carbon dioxide "trail" to its next blood meal.

Male mosquitoes have fuzzy **antennae**. Females do not. The long hairs on the males' antennae help them find female mosquitoes because these hairs are very sensitive to the female mosquitoes' hum.

If a jar has been set up to rear larvae for the purpose of learning about mosquitoes, then adult mosquitoes should be emerging within a couple of weeks. When this happens, the newly emerged adults will perch on the side of the jar and on the underside of the screen over the mouth of the jar. Compare the differences between the males and the females.

Parts of Adult Mosquito

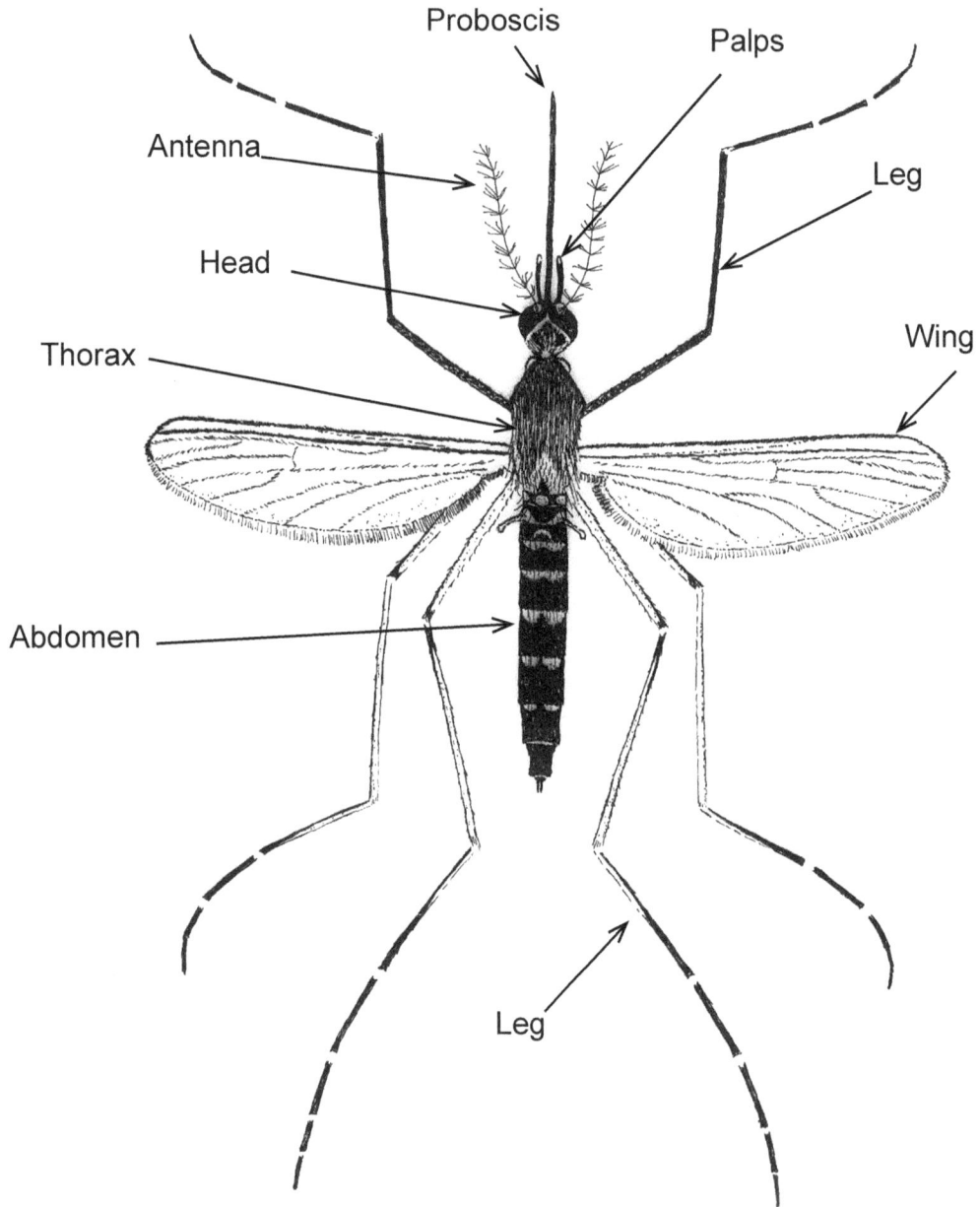

Proboscis

Palps

Antenna

Leg

Head

Thorax

Wing

Abdomen

Leg

Mosquito Ecology and Behaviour

Ecology is the study of how plants and animals live within their environment. The environment includes both living and non-living components. Ecologists who study mosquitoes want to find out how the different mosquitoes live, eat, mate and grow in their habitats and how they affect and are affected by other organisms, temperature, rainfall, food availability and many other factors.

mangrove lagoon

All mosquitoes must spend part of their lives in an aquatic habitat. However, not all species of mosquitoes will be found in the same kind of habitats. Each species of mosquito has typical habitats that are preferred.

Mosquitoes might be found in lagoons, ponds, lakes, rivers and streams. Indeed, larvae can be found around the grassy edges of ponds and lakes. You might find mosquitoes growing in the quiet pools within a stream. But many mosquitoes will be found breeding in other kinds of habitats. These other habitats may not even be noticed by most people.

Stagnant ditches are favourite breeding spots. You can also find mosquitoes in tree holes, clogged gutters, or flowerpots that hold water. Junk cars, used tires, old washing machines, water tanks, livestock troughs, and even your dog's water bowl often provide good mosquito breeding habitats. Low areas that may hold water after a rain can raise many mosquitoes. Even though low spots may be dry, notice the kind of plants growing there: **cattails, arrow plants, water lillies, and bulrush** indicate a **wetland** site and potential source of floodwater mosquitoes.

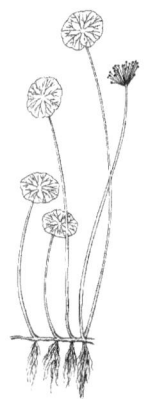

cattails   arrow plants   water lillies

Grouping Mosquitoes by Breeding Habitat

Mosquito species are sometimes placed into groups based on the type of breeding **habitats** they use. These habitat groups include permanent water bodies, flooded areas, and containers. A mosquito species is usually adapted to living in a certain kind of habitat but not in others. These different habitats require different survival tactics.

The **permanent water group** uses habitats such as freshwater marshes, swamps, lakes and ponds that are very stable. They hold water for long periods of time. The water level does not change very fast. These sites often have well-established communities of plants and animals. Permanent water habitats are also often populated by many mosquito predators. Larvae must avoid predators, often by hiding in vegetation and **detritus**. Mosquitoes found in these water bodies lay their eggs on the surface of the water. The larvae generally grow slowly. Their population numbers are usually stable during the warm months. Many mosquitoes in the genera *Anopheles, Mansonia, Coquillettidia* and *Culex* are permanent water breeders.

The mosquitoes in the **floodwater group** lay their eggs on soil that is likely to flood during a good rain. These eggs can remain dry for a long time. When the ground does flood, however, many of the eggs will hatch quickly, sometimes in minutes. These mosquitoes must grow fast before the water dries up. Temporary habitats have few predators to eat mosquito larvae. Adult mosquitoes may begin to emerge within a week or ten days of hatching. Population numbers of these mosquitoes increase greatly a week or two after flooding. Flooded pastures, dry ditches, and tidal marshes are floodwater habitats. A rice field is an example of a man-made floodwater habitat. Mosquitoes belonging to this group include the salt marsh mosquito and the dark rice field mosquito, as well as many *Aedes* species.

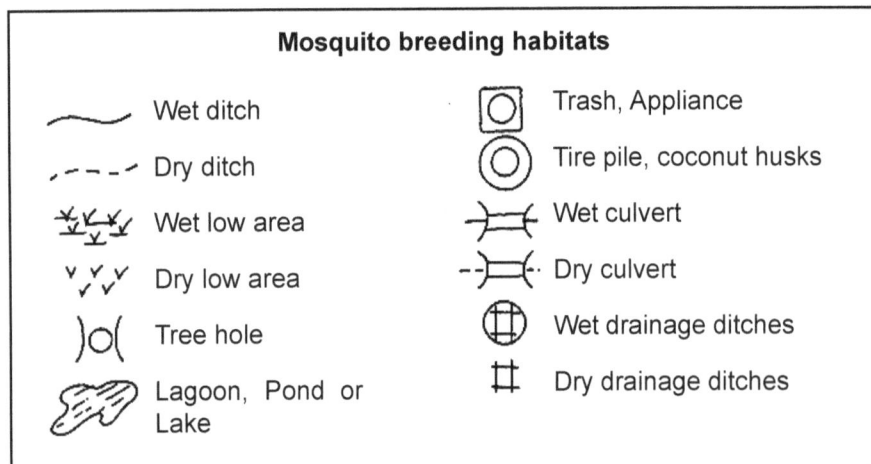

Mosquito breeding habitats

- Wet ditch
- Dry ditch
- Wet low area
- Dry low area
- Tree hole
- Lagoon, Pond or Lake
- Trash, Appliance
- Tire pile, coconut husks
- Wet culvert
- Dry culvert
- Wet drainage ditches
- Dry drainage ditches

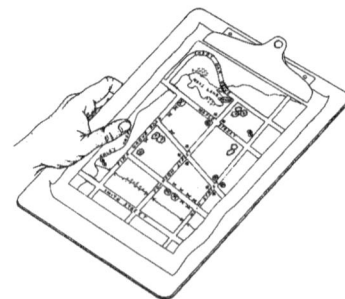

mapping mosquito breeding habitats

A large group of mosquitoes fall into the **artificial and plant container group**. Containers may be natural, such as tree holes, leaf axils, and bromeliads; or containers may be artificial, which includes tires, bottles, cans, Styrofoam cups, old appliances, and any other garbage that will hold water long enough for mosquitoes to hatch, develop and emerge as adults. These habitats may be temporary and dry out after a week or two. An example may be a paper cup or a coconut husk. Some may last for years, such as an old tire or a discarded washing machine.

Mosquitoes breed in polluted water, man-made containers, and trash.

gutters, drains filled with leaves

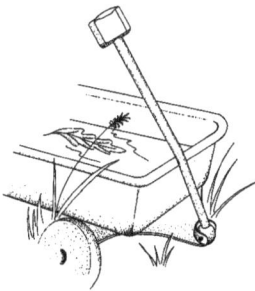

jars, bottles, barrells, cans, Styrofoam containers

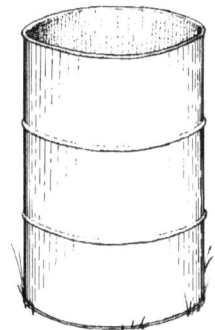

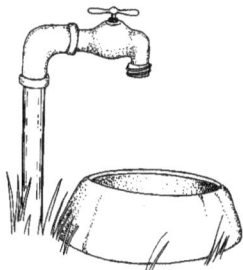

discarded old toys, old appliances

polluted drainage ditches

leaky faucets

discarded old tires, old coconut husks

Hidden Habitats

Many mosquitoes need just a little water in which to grow. Tiny water worlds can be found in strange and interesting places.

Bromeliads are flowering plants that grow on trees in warm, moist environments. Tiny pools of rainwater collect in the leaf axils of certain species. Some bromeliads may hold several gallons of water. Bromeliads form very stable aquatic habitats because they usually live a long time. These pools are important sources of water for many tree dwelling animals. Some animals spend part or all of their lives in these treetop ponds. These natural containers often contain mosquito predators. Dragonfly naiads, beetle larvae, water bugs, fly larvae, tadpoles and even small crabs have been found in bromeliads.

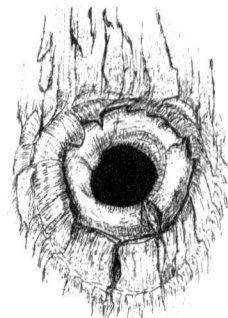

Bromeliads

Tree hole Habitat

Over two hundred species of mosquitoes lay their eggs in bromeliad pools. Some of these mosquitoes are vectors of malaria, yellow fever, dengue fever and other diseases. A single tree can support many bromeliads. A single bromeliad can grow hundreds of mosquitoes. Imagine the number of mosquitoes that can be found in the tree-tops of a tropical forest. Many of these mosquitoes are controlled by predators that share their habitat. Many types of plants hold water and harbour aquatic communities, including mosquitoes. Pitcher plants, axils of banana leaves, heliconia plants, and certain kinds of palms are examples.

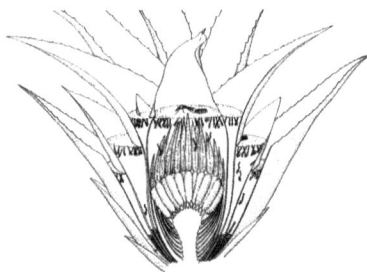

Tank Bromeliads hold liters of water. Many mosquitoes can be produced within these aquatic habitats within the tropical forest canopies.

Water can accumulate in the sections of large bamboo. Water will seep into these chambers through holes bored by beetle larvae.

Larvae in bamboo.

Along the coastal areas of Belize the giant land crab, *Cardisoma guanhumi*, as well as several other crab species, dig holes in the mangroves and beach areas that go down to the water table. These holes are breeding sites for crabhole mosquitoes in the genus *Deinocerites*. The female mosquitoes feed mainly on bird blood, but sometimes bite humans as well. They are not vectors of diseases but can be pests.

Looking at Mosquito Communities

A **community** is made up of all the plants, animals, protozoans, bacteria, fungi, and viruses that live in a habitat. Mosquitoes share their habitats with many different organisms, and some of them greatly affect mosquito populations. Some animals are predators. Some plants help protect larvae from predators. Other animals compete with larvae for food. The water is full of many kinds of microscopic life that serve as food, and sometimes pathogens, of mosquito larvae.

Communities develop in stages. This succession within a new water body begins when bacteria and algae start to grow. Those organisms that can grow without rich nutrients move into a new habitat first, transported by wind, and by birds, and other organisms. Many mosquito larvae, adapted to such habitats, are introduced when gravid female mosquitoes lay their eggs. Algae and diatoms can capture sunlight, take up carbon dioxide, and make sugars through photosynthesis. They can build up quickly in a new habitat. Soon other organisms move in and feed on the first organisms. Gradually the community becomes more complex as new organisms invade the aging habitat and early colonizers become reduced, some probably dying out. If the new habitat lasts long enough, it may reach a stable phase of development where changes occur more slowly.

Adult mosquitoes emerge from their pupal skins, perch upon the surface of the water until their wings fully extend and dry, and then fly away, usually into nearby vegetation to rest and mate, often clinging to the undersides of leaves, or sometimes mating in swarms flying above the water or vegetation. Male mosquitoes siphon juices and saps from the softer stems and leaves of plants. Many female mosquitoes may also take such meals. However, the female begins her search for a blood meal soon after mating. She can detect and follow the carbon dioxide trails we and other animals release when exhaling, finding a host and the promise of a blood meal at the end of the trail. Blood is very nutrient rich and high in protein. This provides the substances that the female mosquitoes need to produce eggs.

What Do Mosquito Larvae Eat?

Mosquito larvae are filter feeders, rapidly moving their fine mouth bristles to create tiny currents of water that sweep particles of organic material and microscopic organisms into these bristles. As water passes through the bristles, many of the fine particles and organisms are sieved out and consumed. Mosquito larvae can also graze on organic films growing on rocks, plants, the sides of containers, and even on the underside of the water's surface. If a mosquito rearing jar was set up as previously suggested, carefully watch larvae as they move and feed.

A mosquito larva's diet depends on the kind of habitat in which it lives. Larvae hanging from the surface of a sunny habitat may be filtering small diatoms from the water. Perhaps they are collecting tiny protozoans swimming near the surface. The mosquito habitat may have many tiny organic particles suspended in the water. Bacteria and fungi may grow on the surface of those particles. Larvae can eat these particles and digest the organisms living on them.

When mosquito larvae graze on plant stems, container bottoms or other underwater surfaces, they are scrapping off the thin living film, or **biofilm**, growing on these surfaces. This film is made up of bacteria and the materials they extrude. Many kinds of attached fungi, stalked and freely moving protozoans, and very small invertebrates may also grow on these submerged sites. These tiny organisms and others are found in every kind of mosquito breeding site, with bacteria, fungi and protozoans being among the first organisms to "colonize" new habitats. These microscopic creatures can reproduce very fast, growing not only on underwater surfaces, but living as plankton in the water column, often attached to suspended organic particles. These organisms provide mosquito larvae with a stable and abundant food supply in whatever water body they may be growing. Usually there is no shortage of food in larval habitats.

Usually there is no shortage of food in larvae habitats.

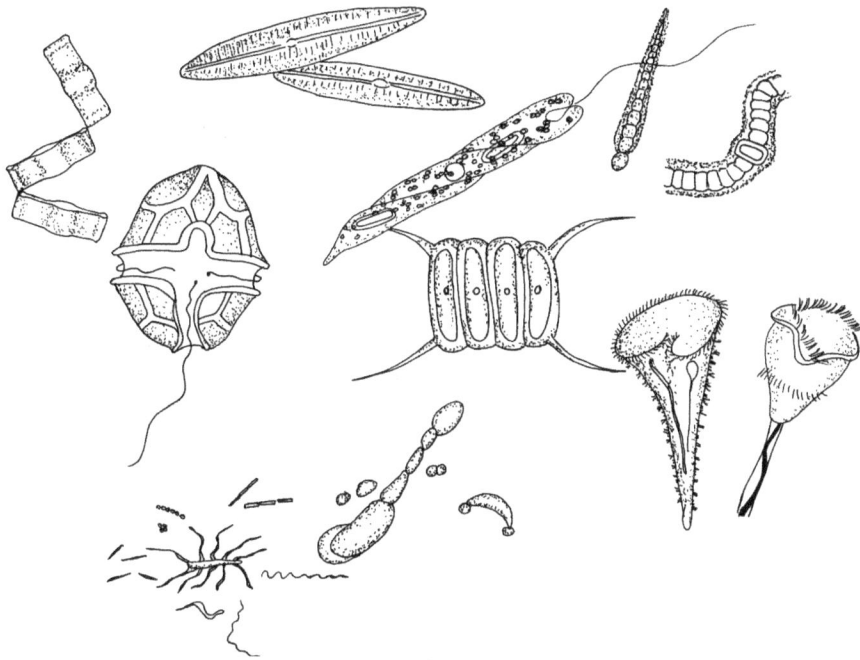

Bioflim is a living film of bacteria and other associated organisms. These include aquatic fungi, diatoms, protozoans and microscopic invertebrates.

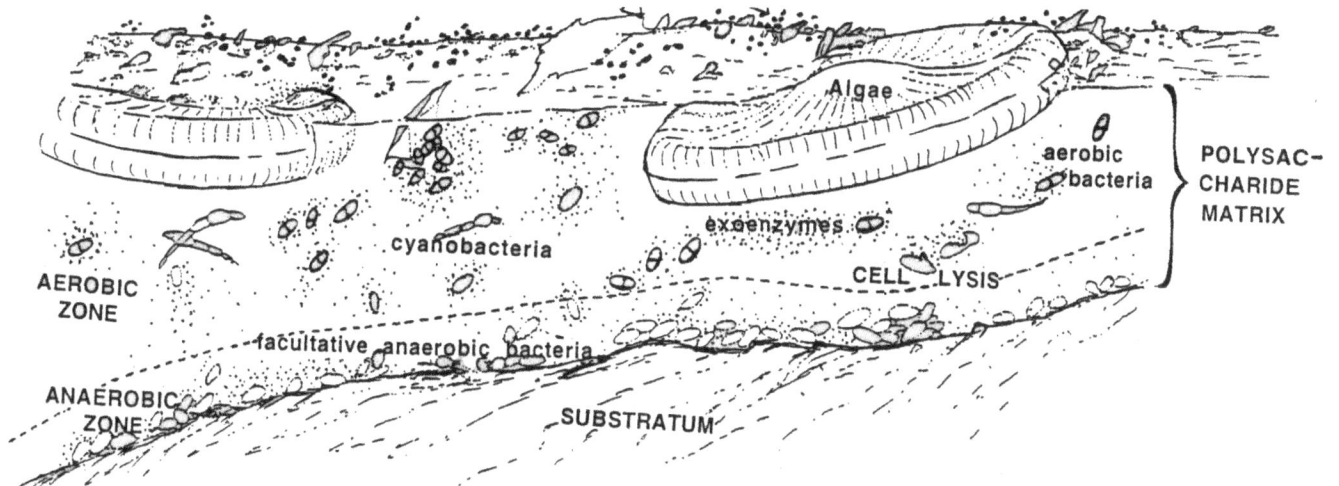

Mosquito larvae filter out microscopic organisms from the water or scrape them off of submerged substrates.

21

Surface Tension

A **water strider** can skate across the surface of a pond. **Springtails** hop like fleas on the water's surface. A pond snail can crawl on the underside of this very thin surface. A mosquito larva can hang suspended from the surface of the water and rest or feed. An emerging adult mosquito can stand on the surface of the water as it pulls its abdomen from its pupal skin. How can this be?

The water surface covers a quiet pond like a tight "skin". This skin is elastic. It stretches and bends under the weight of a pond spider's foot or the weight of a **dyticid beetle** larvae. The **surface tension** forms ripples when a pebble is thrown into the water. To enter the water, a small animal must actually break through the water surface.

Small animals can hang from the surface film and rest, rather than having to constantly swim.

What is this skin and how is it formed?

Water molecules are strongly attracted to each other. At the surface of the pond, water molecules are also strongly repelled by air molecules. This makes the water molecules squeeze closer and attach together right at the surface. Water molecules below the surface are not shoved together so tightly. They have more room to move around than water molecules on the surface. These crowded surface molecules stick together to form a kind of film over the body of water, which is called "surface tension".

The water surface is a special kind of **microhabitat** where certain types of plants and animals live. Concentrations of bacteria and protozoa are found associated with the surface film. This represents rich food resources for mosquito larvae. Many animals that spend their lives on top of the water's surface are too small or weak to break through the surface film. Springtails and water striders are examples of these animals. They are covered with special hairs or skin surfaces that repel water molecules. Should they become swept beneath the surface in a splash, they would be unable to escape through the film and would drown.

Many animals become trapped on this film. Flies that land on the film and are pushed over by a gust of wind may become stuck. Their wings are not equipped with a lot of tiny water repelling hairs. Unable to pull themselves free, they become easy prey for the water strider. Mosquitoes trying to emerge from pupal skins can suffer the same fate. That is the reason most mosquitoes are found in quiet, still waters that are protected from the wind.

Many tiny animals can hang from the surface film. A mosquito larva is a good example. Larvae are heavier than water. If a mosquito larva stops swimming beneath the water, it slowly begins to sink. But it can attach to the surface film and not have to swim, saving valuable energy. Water repellent hairs grow around the end of a mosquito larva's breathing siphon on the tip of its abdomen, or on the head end of a pupa. When the larva or pupa

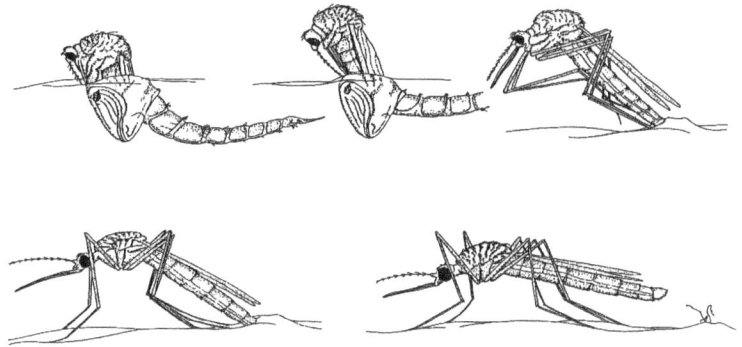

Once it emerges from the pupal skin, the adult mosquito must be able to stand on the surface film until it's wings dry and it can fly away.

reaches the surface, it opens up the end of its siphon tube. As the tube opens, these hairs protrude and lay against the top of the water's surface. This anchors the mosquito to the surface film.

The larvae of many genera of mosquitoes can be identified by the way they attach to the surface film and the structure of their siphons. *Culex* and *Aedes* mosquito larvae have long breathing siphons and hang from the surface film with their heads down. *Anopheles* larvae do not have long siphons and attach to the surface film with hairs along their bodies, lying horizontally against the underside of the water surface.

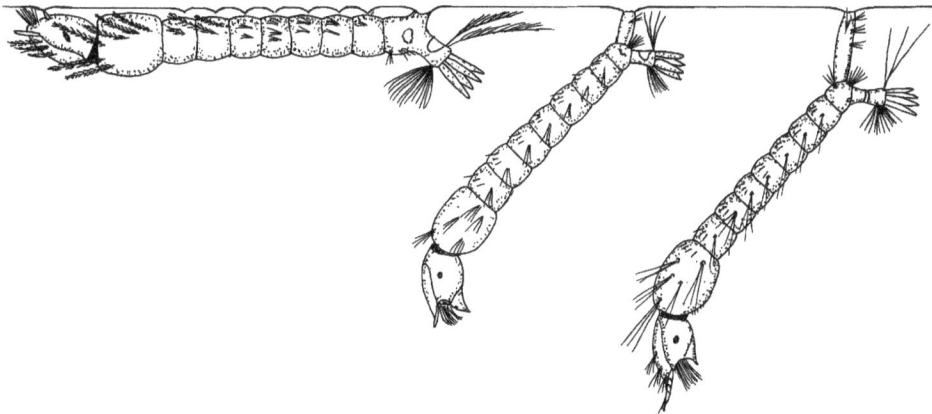

(left) *Anopheles* larvae lie flat against the surface of the water because they have no siphon

(middle) *Aedes* larvae hang with their heads down and have only one tuft of hairs on their siphons.

(right) *Culex* larvae hang with their heads down and have more than one tuft of hairs on their siphons..

The Mosquito and the Botfly

Human botflies (*Dermatobia hominis*) are important pests in many parts of the world. Larvae or "bots" of these parasitic flies wiggle into the skin of their hosts through a skin follicle. They form a chamber within the skin in which they live and grow, maintaining an opening in the surface of the skin through which they breath. The larvae feed on living skin tissue. When they are ready to change into pupae they wiggle out through the breathing pore and fall to the ground.

The wound appears to be a small mosquito bite at first. But it does not heal. Instead it becomes larger and eventually the host feels little pricks as the larvae feeds and squirms. It usually takes a couple of weeks to begin really noticing the larva. Tourists returning from infected locations often have no idea what has gotten under their skin.

Botfly larva is very small when it first hatches out, small enough to enter a skin pore. The larva lives with its head down and breathes through the tip of its abdomen that it extends through the hole in the skin. Within a month they can grow to the thickness of a pencil. Rows of stiff spines help keep the larva from being easily removed from the skin of the host. Botflies infect not only humans, but many species of wildlife and domestic animals. They leave a large open sore in the skin that may become infected. Botfly wounds are a favourite entry point for screw worms (another parasitic fly) and other infectious agents.

The botfly is a big noisy flier and can be driven away easily. So how does the female botfly deposit her larvae on the skin of her victim? She uses another insect as a vector. Although flies and sometimes even ticks are used, mosquitoes are the best vectors for botfly larvae. The female botfly will catch a female mosquito and, holding it within her legs, glue her eggs to the underside of her captive. When it is released, the mosquito finds its next host and lands to feed. The warmth of the host's skin stimulates the botfly larvae and they squirm out of their eggs. When they fall on the skin of the host they quickly begin to burrow into an available pore.

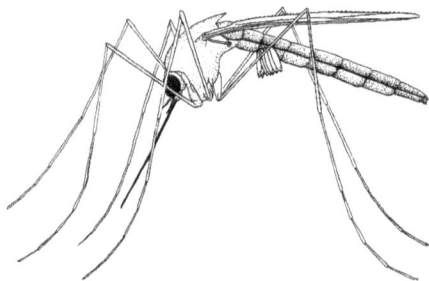

Mosquito with botfly eggs glued to the underside of her abdomen

Human Botfly Larvae

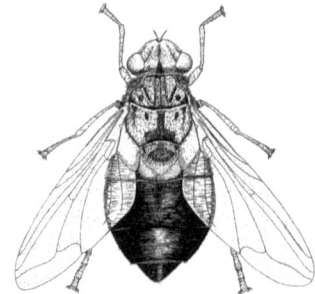

Human Botfly Adult

Mosquitoes that Travel Around the World

Some mosquitoes have moved around the world. They have crossed mountains, deserts and oceans. They have travelled from one continent to another. But how have such fragile insects managed this feat? How did they survive these long journeys? They were carried by people. They travelled in caravans, wagons, ships and planes.

Thousands of years ago, in the Old World, certain species of mosquito moved from the forest into villages. They laid their eggs in water jugs and took blood meals from the people and their domestic animals. They became domestic mosquitoes. The yellow fever mosquito is a prime example.

In the eighteenth century, European explorers were busy exploring and exploiting the new world. They crossed the vast ocean in wooden ships. They carried large barrels of fresh water to drink during the long passage. In these barrels they also carried the eggs and larvae of yellow fever mosquitoes. Thus this tiny, delicate insect came to the new world as a stowaway.

Truck tire casings are expensive to make. Often when the tread is worn away, old tire casings are saved and fitted with new tread. Re-treaded tires are much cheaper to buy than new tires. Tire dealers in the United States buy hundreds of thousands of old tires from Taiwan, Japan and other countries abroad. These old tires are preferred as cores for recapped tires because these tires are made with natural rubber and last much longer than tires made only from synthetic rubber in the United States.

A population of Asian tiger mosquitoes was found in Houston, Texas in 1985. It was soon realized that this mosquito came to this hemisphere from the Far East. They were transported in containers of old tire casings brought to the United States from Asia to be re-treaded. Since then, the Asian tiger mosquito has moved across the United States. It travelled in trucks loaded with old tires being moved from one part of the country to another. Its invading populations often became established along the interstate highway system. These mosquitoes have now moved into Mexico and Central America.

Today, passenger and cargo planes travel to every country in the world. Often insects board these planes and are also carried to other parts of the world. Many of these insects are mosquitoes. Most of these insects probably die before they can settle into a new home. But how many manage to survive? What will happen when a certain insect becomes established in another country? Will it infect people, livestock, or wildlife with disease agents? How will it adjust to the plant and animal communities in its new home? How will native communities adapt to this new resident? Only time and close observation can find these answers.

Identifying Mosquitoes

When you spot a mosquito, try to determine if it is a male or a female. Remember, male mosquitoes have fuzzy antennas while females do not. Males use their extra sensitive antennae to locate the hum of females.

Identify the genus of the mosquitoes you are finding. You can distinguish the three main genera of mosquitoes you are likely to see, *Aedes, Culex* and *Anopheles,* by their resting positions. *Anopheles* mosquitoes rest with their **abdomens** pointed upward. *Aedes* mosquitoes crouch low against the surface. The head, **thorax** and abdomen form a straight line. *Culex* mosquitoes do not crouch as low. Generally their body is bent, forming an angle.

Adult Mosquito Resting Positions

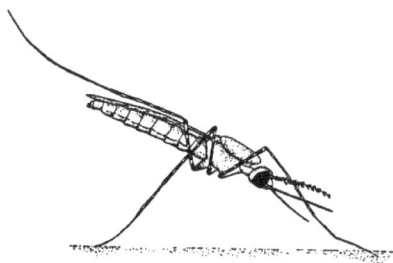

Anopheles

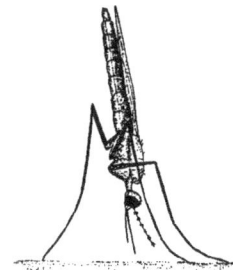

Anopheles

Aedes

Culex

Mosquito Look-A-Likes

Sometimes people confuse mosquitoes with other kinds of flies. Often when people describe mosquitoes as being "as big as a butterfly but did not bite", chances are they saw a crane fly. Non-biting midges are often mistaken for mosquitoes. When in doubt, look for the snout. Mosquitoes have a long narrow proboscis. If your specimen does not have a proboscis, then it is something other than a mosquito.

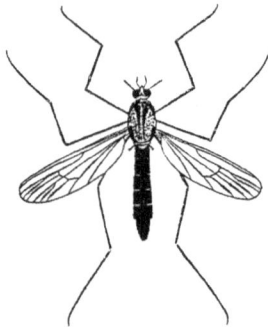

Dixid Midge, *Dixidae*   Non-biting Midge, *Chironomidae*   Crane Fly, *Tipulidae*

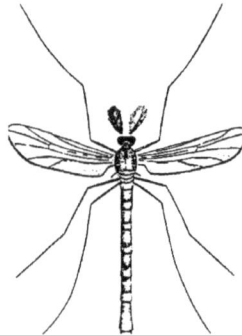

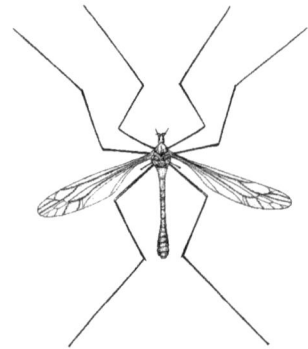

Mosquito Identification

More than 2,500 different species of mosquitoes have been described from around the world. They are true flies in the order *Diptera*, having only one pair of wings. The second pair of wings have been reduced to knob-shaped **halteres** attached to the thorax just behind the first pair of wings. All mosquitoes belong to the family *Culicidae*, characterized as flies that have aquatic larvae and as adults having mouthparts developed for piercing and sucking. They also differ from many other flies in having scales on their bodies and wings.

Those mosquitoes that are important to humans, those that bite us or our livestock and that carry diseases which affect people, typically have a common name such as the "southern house mosquito". Many mosquitoes are known only to **entomologists** who study them and do not have common names. However each described mosquito species is given a unique **scientific name**, such as *Culex quinquefaciatus* for the southern house mosquito. In this example *Culex*, the first name listed, is the genus and is always capitalized. The second name, *quinquefaciatus*, is the species and is not capitalized. Both names are listed together and are *italicized*, or underlined if hand written.

New species are being found as new habitats are being explored. The job of identifying mosquito species is a special skill. An entomologist who specializes in identifying and describing new mosquito species is a mosquito **taxonomist**. Some mosquito taxonomists write **taxonomic keys**. These keys are essential guide books that help other entomologists and mosquito control technicians identify particular mosquito species. Taxonomic keys use differences in body structures to sort mosquitoes into different genera, subgenera, species and sometimes sub-species. Mosquitoes in one genus share certain structures that are not found in mosquitoes belonging to another genus. For instance, *Anopheles* mosquitoes have very long palps. Other mosquitoes do not. These long palps are a "key" characteristic used to identify mosquitoes in the genus *Anopheles*.

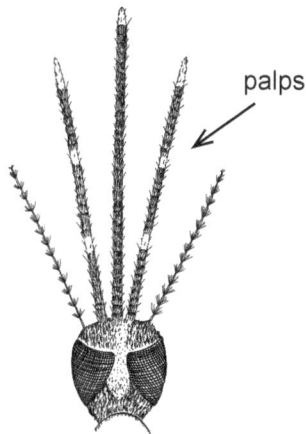

palps

Head of female *Anopheles* mosquito showing long palps

There are many different mosquito species, but typically only a certain number of species are found in certain places. Some villages, towns, and even cities will have only three or four problem mosquito species, while urban areas may have many more. There are 112 mosquito species, representing 17 different genera that have been found in Belize, but generally only a dozen or so species cause problems for humans, pets, and livestock.

Six Important Mosquitoes

The following are profiles of mosquitoes having public health importance in Belize. These selected mosquitoes also serve to represent the diversity of mosquitoes that vary in their life cycles, habitat preferences, and behaviour patterns. They also demonstrate the kinds of characteristics used to tell one species from another. Most of taxonomic features shown here can be seen with the unaided eye, or at most a 5X magnifying lens.

Malaria Mosquito (*Anopheles darlingi*)

Description: This is a light brown mosquito with:

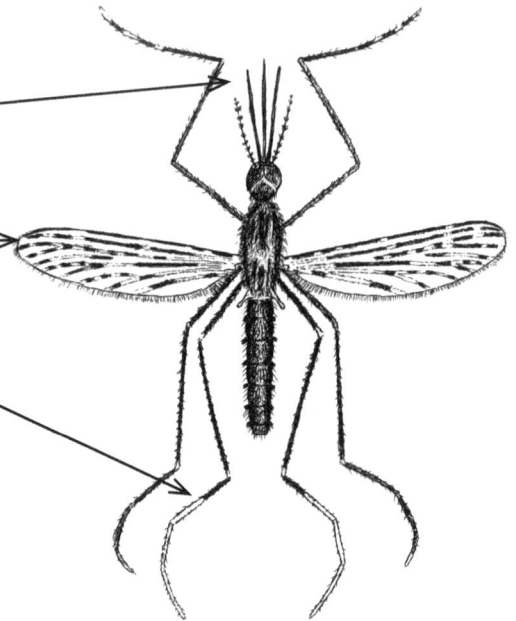

A. palps that are almost as long as the proboscis

B. dark spots on the wings

C. white tarsi on the hind legs.

Breeding Habitat: This is a riverine mosquito found largely in rural lowland forest areas. Larval habitats are typically natural bodies of water, including, pools, swamps, lakes, lagoons, and especially slow flowing, shaded streams and rivers with clear, unpolluted water containing submersed vegetation and overhanging spiny bamboo. Larvae are often found in floating debris patches along river margins. Deforestation tends to promote favorable breeding sites for *Anopheles darling*.

Life Cycle: As do other *Anopheles* mosquitoes, this species lays single eggs on the surface of the water, each egg equipped with small lateral floats. In streams and rivers habitat areas are flushed out during high flows in the rainy season.

Biting Behaviour: This mosquito tends to bite all night with biting rates showing significant increases in areas that are deforested. They feed outdoors and indoors, but tend to rest outdoors. However, the behaviour of this mosquito varies from place to place, possibly as an adaptation to differences in human behaviour, including mosquito control tactics.

Flight Range: It has been shown to fly several miles, entering houses located well away from rivers and streams.

Importance: *Anopheles darling,* found in Mexico and throughout most countries of Central and South America, is one of the most important vectors of malaria in the Neotropics. It is also thought to be a vector of human filarial diseases, having transmitted *Wuchereria bancrofti* in the laboratory and with some collected specimens being naturally infected with this nematode parasite.

Yellow Fever Mosquito (*Aedes aegypti*)

Description: This small mosquito is dark brown to black with silver-white markings:

Breeding Habitat: It is found almost exclusively in shaded artificial containers around houses and buildings, including tires, cans, jars, flower pots, and gutters.

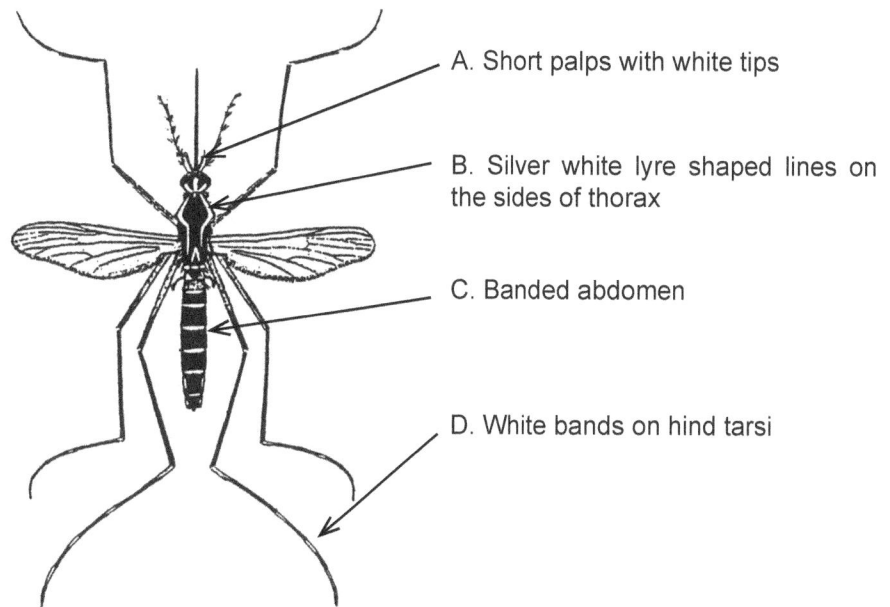

A. Short palps with white tips

B. Silver white lyre shaped lines on the sides of thorax

C. Banded abdomen

D. White bands on hind tarsi

Life Cycle: Single eggs are laid on the inside surfaces of containers at or above the waterline or occasionally on the water surface. The eggs can resist drying for up to several months. Flooded eggs can hatch in two or three days at high temperatures. Under good conditions, larval development is completed in 10 to 12 days. Cool weather lengthens the development period. The pupa stage lasts about two days.

Biting Behaviour: It usually bites during the morning or late afternoon. It prefers human blood meals, biting principally around ankles, back of the neck and under sleeves. It enters houses readily.

Flight Range: 100 to 300 feet

Importance: This mosquito is a vector of urban yellow fever, dengue, chikungunya, and the recently introduced Zika virus. It is also a significant pest species. It exists as a completely domestic mosquito within the Western Hemisphere. It breeds solely in artificial containers, raised by its primary host—humans. It is thought to have been introduced to this hemisphere by the early European explorers crossing oceans with their drinking water and *A. aegypti* (at least its eggs) sealed in barrels. Once in the New World, *A. aegypti* found a niche within artificial containers that it was aptly suited to occupy.

Asian Tiger Mosquito (*Aedes albopictus*)

Description: This mosquito is very similar in appearance to the yellow fever mosquito. It is dark brown to black with silver white markings:

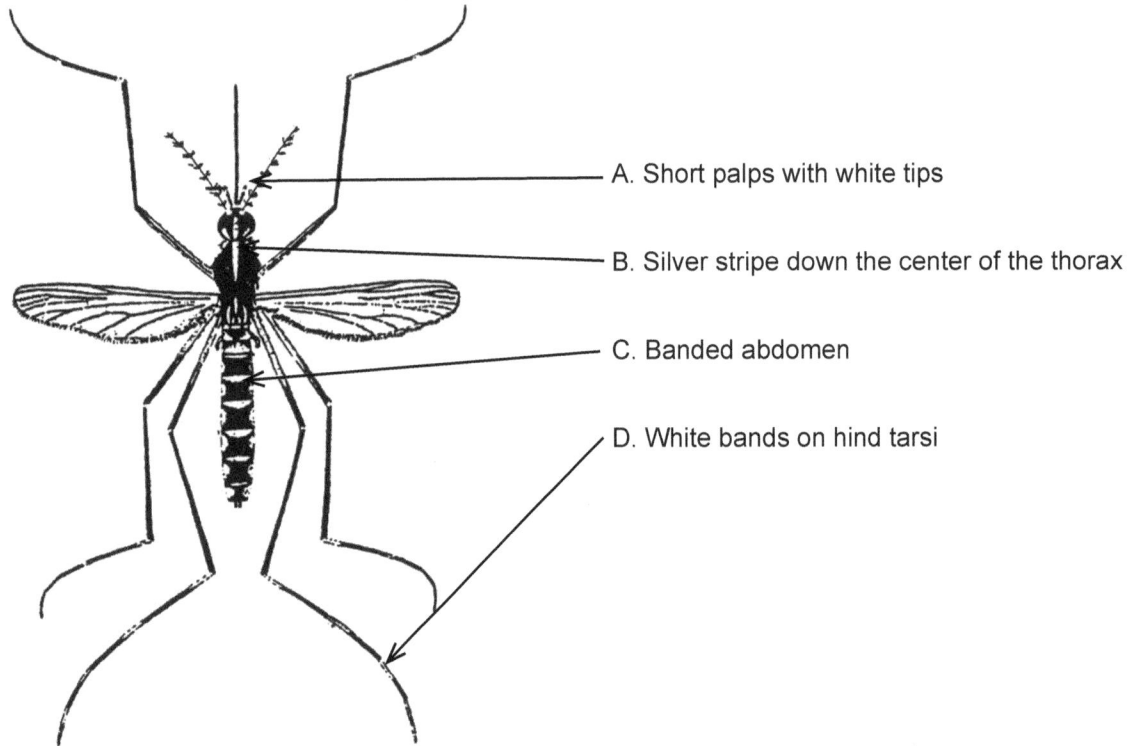

A. Short palps with white tips

B. Silver stripe down the center of the thorax

C. Banded abdomen

D. White bands on hind tarsi

Breeding Habitat: Artificial containers, especially used tires, are the prime breeding sites. This mosquito has moved into tree holes in the some of its new range, making it an extremely difficult mosquito to control.

Life cycle: Little is known about this mosquito in our area. However, its life cycle may be similar to that of the yellow fever mosquito.

Biting Behaviour: This is an aggressive biter, attacking soon after you encounter a breeding area. Often these mosquitoes land and bite immediately.

Flight range: Less than quarter of a mile.

Seasonal occurrence: The strain of Asian tiger mosquito introduced into the Western Hemisphere is believed to have originated from the temperate orient and can survive cold temperatures better than the yellow fever mosquito. They are active during much of the year. The eggs go into an inactive state called "diapause" in October or November within colder parts of its range and remain dormant until spring. This mosquito was introduced into the southern United States, first showing up in Houston, Texas, in the late 1980s. It was believed to have been originally brought into California as eggs within shipping containers loaded with old truck tire casings. The containers were placed on trucks and taken to a tire yard in Houston. Tires were removed, sorted and stacked in the outdoors, where they collected rainwater. Eggs exposed to the water hatched and a new species of mosquito was successfully introduced into the United States. The females quickly found blood meals and laid eggs in many of the thousands of tires. Many of these tires were sold to other used tire dealers, often being shipped across the country. Thus within one year, this new species spread from the Pacific coast to the Atlantic coast. *A. albopictus* was first found in Belize in 2011 and this new mosquito is now a permanent resident. It seems to compete with *A. aegypti* for breeding sites, is a more fierce biter (hence its name!) and serves as a vector for more diseases.

Importance: The Asian tiger mosquito can carry yellow fever, dengue fever, and possibly chikungunya, Zika and several encephalitis viruses. Laboratory studies have shown that this mosquito can carry St. Louis encephalitis, but this has not been demonstrated in the wild. More study is also needed to determine if it can also transmit chikungunya and Zika.

Inland Floodwater Mosquito (*Aedes vexans*)

Description: This is a medium-size brown to golden brown mosquito with light gray or white markings including:

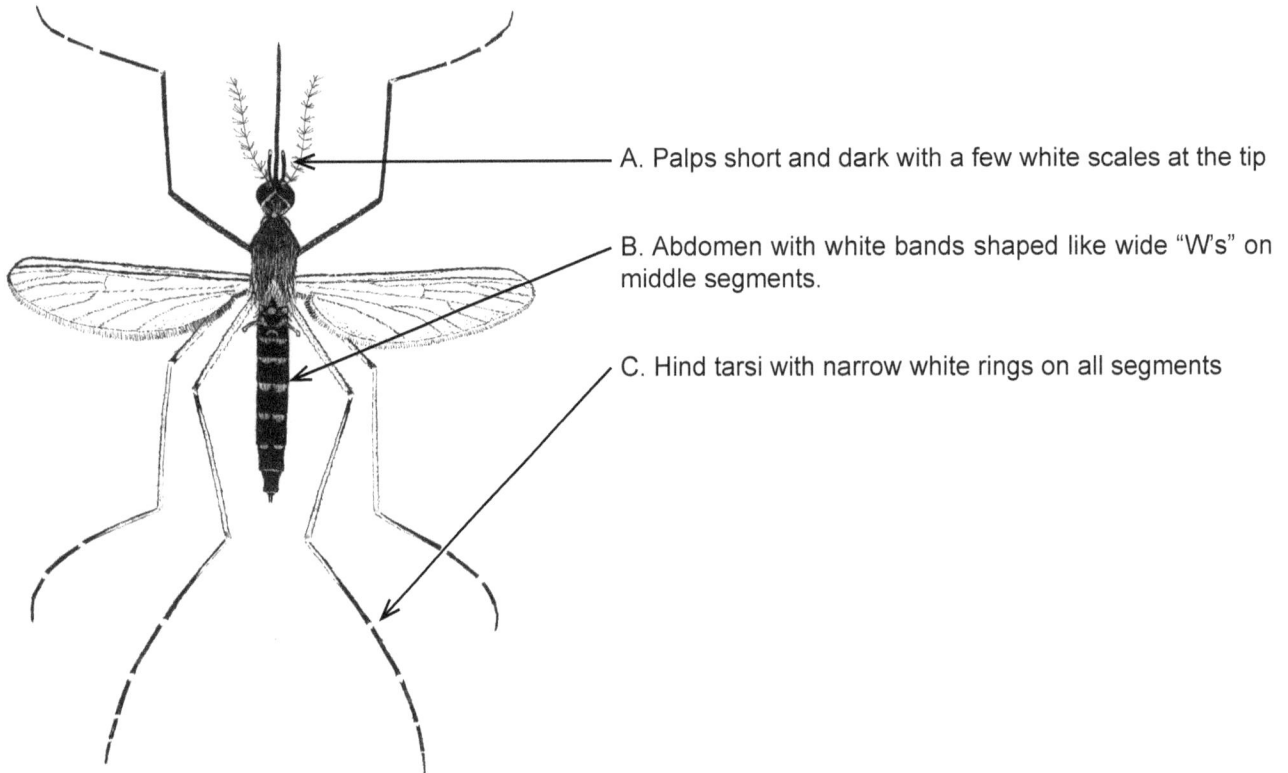

A. Palps short and dark with a few white scales at the tip

B. Abdomen with white bands shaped like wide "W's" on middle segments.

C. Hind tarsi with narrow white rings on all segments

Breeding Habitat: Areas include floodwaters, rain pools and any temporary body of freshwater in both wooded and open areas.

Life Cycle: Many broods are produced per year when breeding areas are flooded by rains. Eggs are laid on the ground and hatch when they are flooded. Aquatic stages require 10 to 21 days to develop, depending on environmental conditions.

Biting Habits: They are vicious biters, being active mainly at dusk and after dark.

Flight Range: 5 to 10 miles on average.

Importance: Pest mosquito, not proven to be a disease vector.

Southern House Mosquito (*Culex quinquefasciatus*)

Description: This is a brown, medium-sized mosquito with white markings, including:

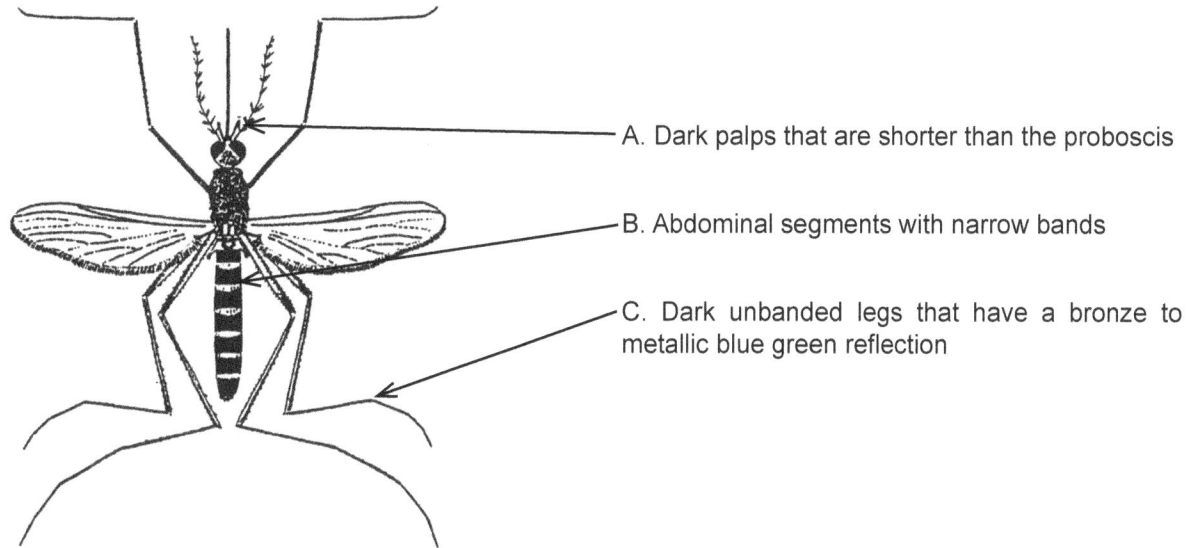

A. Dark palps that are shorter than the proboscis

B. Abdominal segments with narrow bands

C. Dark unbanded legs that have a bronze to metallic blue green reflection

Breeding Habitat: Major breeding sites are waters heavily polluted with organic material such as ditches receiving septic tank overflow, drainage canals, poorly drained ditches, cesspools and polluted ground water. This mosquito will also breed in artificial containers.

Life Cycle: Eggs are laid in floating rafts of 50 to 400, hatching within a day or two in warm temperatures. The aquatic stages are completed in 8 to 10 days. During cooler weather, several weeks may be required for complete development. Generally, breeding is continuous throughout the year.

Biting Behaviour: This mosquito readily enters houses, feeding on humans and domestic animals.

Flight Range: These mosquitoes migrate only short distances unless large numbers are produced.

Importance: It is a major vector of St. Louis encephalitis and may carry dog heart worms and other nematode parasites.

Cannibal Mosquitoes (*Toxorhynchites spp.*)

Description: Slow-flying mosquitoes that are purplish-brown and gold with metallic blue, blue-green and gold markings with:

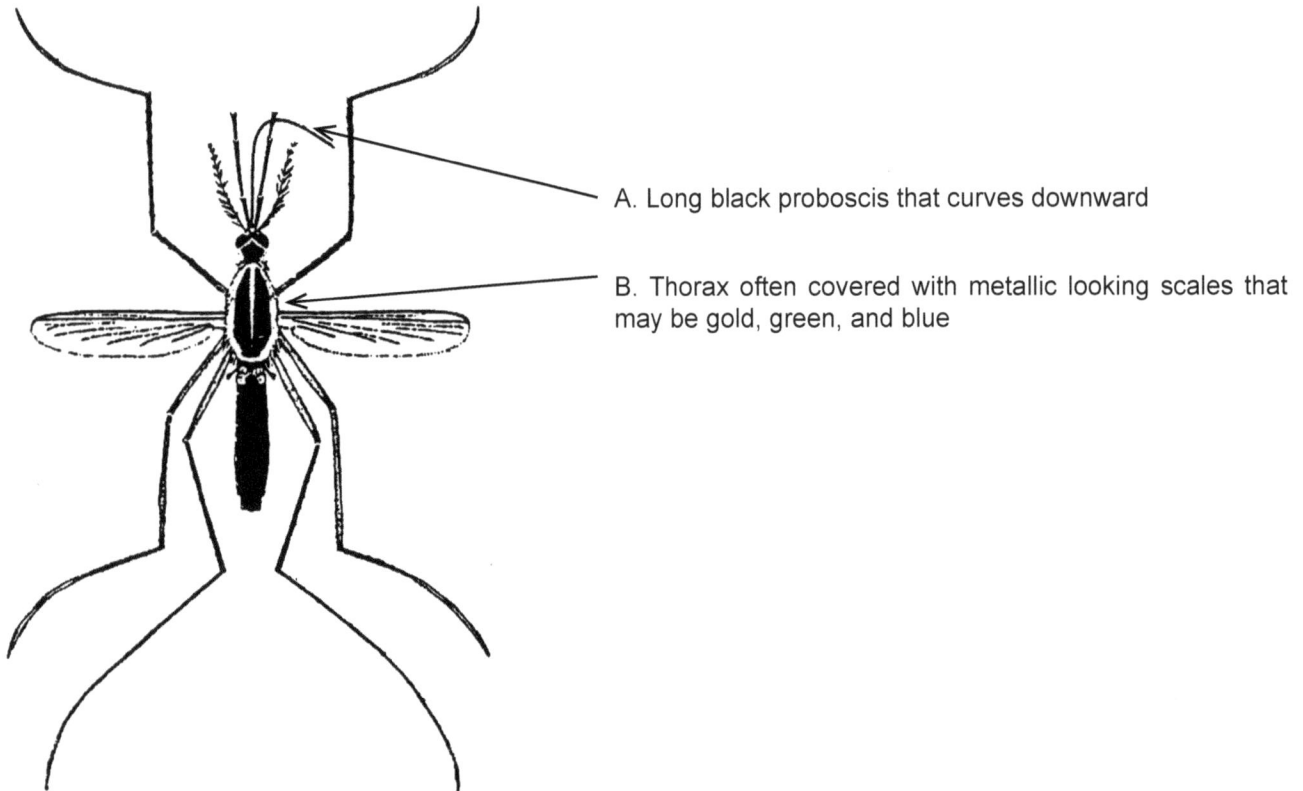

A. Long black proboscis that curves downward

B. Thorax often covered with metallic looking scales that may be gold, green, and blue

Breeding Habitat: Tree holes, bromeliads, and artificial containers are suitable habitats.

Life Cycle: Breeding may occur year round unless water dries up.

Biting Behaviour: These mosquitoes are not blood feeders.

Flight Range: Short.

Importance: Larvae prey on other container-breeding mosquitoes and are being successfully used as biological control agents in some large urban mosquito control programmes.

Mosquito Surveillance and Control

When mosquito numbers begin to increase, often so does the incidence and spread of mosquito-borne diseases. The population of disease-carrying mosquitoes has to be high enough for the disease agent (virus, bacteria, protozoa, nematode) to infect enough mosquitoes to persist. If the population of its mosquito vector is too low, the disease agent will die out and mosquitoes will not be infected and cannot transmit the disease to the host. Most of the mosquitoes that do carry diseases that affect humans are those that we grow right around us. These are the "urban" mosquitoes or "domestic" mosquitoes that breed in the solid waste we haphazardly discard that can collect and hold water, or the sewage-contaminated ditches with stagnant pools, clogged drains and gutters, water vats, deep tire ruts, and many other habitats. If we can control these mosquito populations, keeping their numbers too low for effective disease transmission to occur, we can control the diseases.

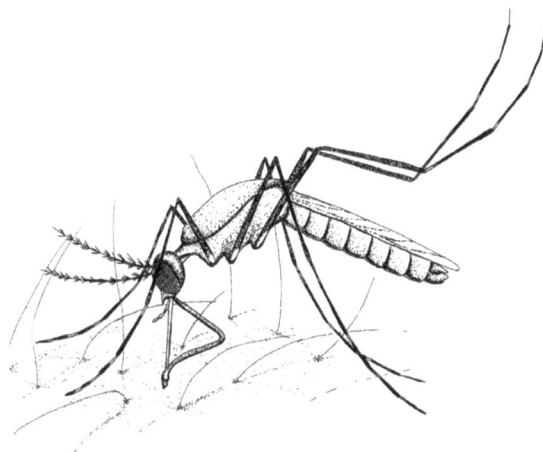

Controlling mosquitoes is a continual job that is often done by an official control agency or department, or at least by trained technicians. However, mosquito control needs the help and cooperation of the community to be effective. It is very important to know the species of mosquitoes that are a potential or actual problem, and understand the biology and ecology of larvae and adults within their different habitats in order to prescribe the best control strategy. Mosquito control technicians have to watch mosquito populations closely in order to know when to apply control methods. They conduct surveys of mosquito adult and larval populations to gather the data needed to decide when and how these populations should be controlled. Technicians also conduct follow-up surveys to determine if their control strategies are working.

Surveying Mosquito Populations within Neighbourhoods

There are several different ways to learn about the mosquito populations within an area. Most of these methods do not require expensive equipment. Conducting routine surveys is a very important aspect of effective mosquito control. The technicians and programme managers must know where mosquitoes are breeding around their villages, towns, and cities. They also must keep watch over mosquito populations, implementing appropriate control efforts only when necessary.

Surveying for adult mosquitoes can be as simple as conducting a landing rate count. Wearing a pair of dark trousers, simply stand still in an area where mosquitoes are active and count the ones that land on the front of your trousers over a three minute interval. A well trained technician can also identify the different species of mosquitoes as they land. Many mosquito control agencies depend on calls from community members alerting them to mosquito activity.

Larvae surveys are very important and can be conducted with some basic tools, such as a long handled dipper to sample around the vegetated edges of stagnant pools, ditches, and other water bodies. A kitchen ladle is a handy sampling device for collecting water from old discarded tires and other containers. A large kitchen baster can be used to siphon water out of hard-to-reach sites used by many mosquito species.

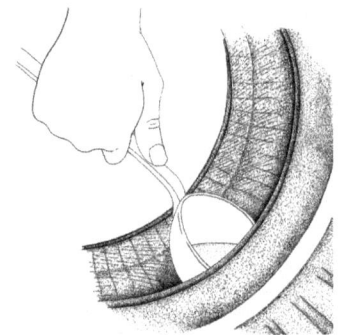

Some mosquito control technicians may sample for eggs laid by mosquitoes as an indication of the level of breeding activity. Yellow fever and Asian tiger mosquitoes seek rough surfaces just above the waterline within containers on which to lay their eggs. They are also drawn to dark places. **Ovitraps** are used to survey for these mosquitoes, which are black plastic cups that are half filled with water and have a strip of stiff, rough paper or a wooden paddle attached to the inside. A hole punched in the side just above the water level ensures that a rain will not completely fill the cup. Female mosquitoes lay their eggs on the rough paper or wood, rather than the smooth side of the cup. Eggs can be counted to help determine reproductive activity.

Female southern house mosquitoes are attracted to foul water, such as a stagnant ditch contaminated with sewage or other organic waste. Sometimes "muck" buckets are stationed around an area to attract egg laying females. A three to five gallon bucket is half filled with water and a little bit of cow or horse manure added to the water to give it an "attractive" odor. The bucket is inspected each day and egg rafts counted and removed. If larvae are found, the bucket is emptied and refilled.

Controlling Mosquito Populations

When mosquito populations begin to build in size, appropriate control strategies can be implemented to reduce their numbers again. Many different methods have been developed to control mosquitoes. Getting rid of breeding habitats will reduce populations of mosquitoes breeding in artificial containers. Natural parasites, pathogens and predators of mosquitoes are being grown and used in many programmes. Chemical pesticides are widely used to kill mosquitoes.

Using Chemicals

Pesticides are chemicals used to kill those organisms deemed to be pests. Those chemicals specifically used to kill insects are called insecticides. Farmers spray insecticides on their crops to kill caterpillars, beetles and other insect pests. Homeowners have their houses treated against termites, roaches and ants. Insecticides are also used to control mosquitoes, with chemicals often being applied by municipal workers trained in the use of pesticides. Insecticides should be used very carefully because they can kill and harm far more than just insects. They must be applied as described on the label. If used incorrectly, insecticides can harm beneficial insects, fish, birds and even humans. **Pesticide applicators** should always read and follow the pesticide label closely, paying close attention to the warning statement and directions for use. Also the label should give instructions on the proper disposal of empty insecticide containers.

Exclusive use of chemicals for mosquito control is not the answer. Mosquitoes often become resistant if an insecticide is used often over a long time period. Therefore, the pesticide no longer works to reduce their numbers. Pesticides may kill mosquito predators, bees and other important insects, because they don't build up a resistance. These same chemicals used to control mosquitoes can also harm people who breathe the pesticide or ingest it by drinking contaminated water. Besides the issues of resistance build up in mosquito populations and potential harm to humans, pesticides also cost a lot to use. Modern mosquito control agencies try to control mosquitoes with other methods than just chemical application. Reducing breeding sites and using biological control agents are some of the ways mosquito numbers can be kept low. However, when mosquito populations become too large or a mosquito borne disease is present, chemicals are used for fast control.

Controlling adult mosquitoes requires spraying neighbourhoods, including not just mosquitoes, but also children, elderly people, pets, roof tops that drain into water vats, and everything else with toxic clouds of pesticides. A typical mosquito spray truck is equipped with an "ultra-low-volume" spray unit that creates a thin mist of pesticide, such as **malathion**. The chemical is broken up into small droplets that drift into adult mosquito habitats. Should one of these **micro-droplets** land on an adult mosquito, it dies. However, the pesticide has the same effect on bees, butterflies, moths, and other creatures. In the earlier days of chemical mosquito control, trucks carried **thermofogger** units that produced thick clouds of "smoke" when a mixture of diesel and pesticide was sprayed onto a hot manifold. These pesticides are applied in the late afternoon and evening when biting mosquitoes are the most active and not hidden in the vegetation.

Chemicals have been developed that mimic a certain growth hormone of mosquitoes. These products offer another tool for mosquito control agencies to use. When introduced into mosquito breeding sites, larvae absorb these chemicals and their normal growth patterns are disrupted. This ultimately results in malformed larvae that eventually die. However, this material also affects other organisms in the water and can have a serious effect on aquatic ecosystems. These products are expensive to use.

Oils have been used to control mosquito breeding in swamps and marshes. Diesel fuel was often used in the early days of malaria control, being poured directly on the surface of the water. Ideally, the oil covers the water's surface and mosquitoes (and everything else) have trouble breaking through the film to breath air. Consequently they suffocate. Many materials used, such as diesel fuel, are very toxic, killing not just mosquito larvae but also many other organisms living in wetlands and backwaters. Less toxic vegetable-based oils and other formulations have been developed that spread across the surface of water as a very thin layer. However, wind can push these surface materials against one side of a lake or open lagoon. Oil will also cling to emergent aquatic plants and become ineffective as a mosquito control agent. Many of these products are expensive.

Using Pathogens

Several bacteria and fungi found naturally infesting mosquito larvae have been tested as possible control agents. These **biological control** agents are often very specific. Many will only affect mosquito larvae. A good biological control agent must be easy to grow. It must remain viable long enough to be shipped, stored and finally applied to breeding sites and do its job. It must be easy to apply. It must not harm other "non-target" aquatic organisms. Of course, the agent must provide good mosquito control. Very few of the many organisms that have been tested meet all of these requirements. Also there is always great concern about the effects of releasing a foreign organism into an ecosystem.

The most widely used bacteria in mosquito control is *Bacillus thuringiensis israelensis*, also known as **Bth-14**. This bacterium was found in a dead mosquito larvae from Israel in 1977. It was isolated, cultivated, and extensively tested on many different kinds of mosquitoes. It is now commercially available and is sold to mosquito control agencies around the world to kill larvae. It is applied as a dead spore that is not capable of reproducing in the environment. Therefore it is not a new species that is being introduced into the ecosystem. Besides mosquitoes, Bth-14 will kill black fly larvae and a few filter-feeding chironomid or non-biting midge larvae, but no other organisms. Black flies are major pests in many areas. They also carry the nematode worm that causes river blindness in the tropics.

Bth-14 spores are swallowed as the larva filter feeds. When spores reach the larva's acidic gut, they burst open and release a poison that kills the cells lining the gut. The gut wall can no longer absorb food and the larva consequently starves. The advantages of using Bt H-14 is that it does not reproduce in the wild, it does not kill natural predators, and it is usually highly effective in controlling mosquito larvae.

Using Predators

Many different kinds of animals prey on mosquitoes in their natural habitats. Some animals select mosquitoes over other kinds of prey. Other predators are more general feeders.

Some of these predators have been used in mosquito control programmes. The mosquito fish, *Gambusia affinis*, has proven to be a very effective predator of mosquito larvae. They have been used in mosquito control programmes and introduced into many tropical and temperate freshwater ecosystems around the world. Although they are effective mosquito control agents, they eat many other organisms and this aggressive mosquito fish can out-compete other local species in those ecosystems in which it is introduced. It is generally better to utilize local mosquito predators rather than introducing a new species into local communities.

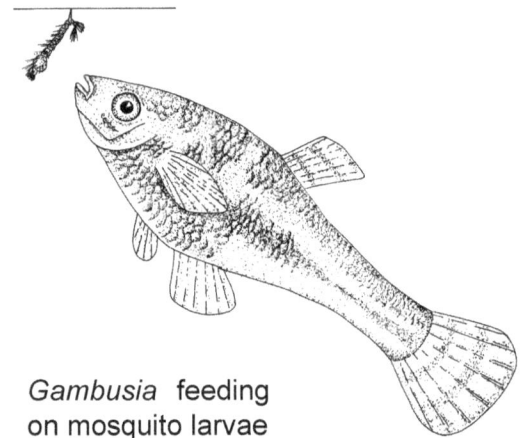

Gambusia feeding on mosquito larvae

Planarians are familiar to most biology students. These flat worms are well known for their ability to regenerate lost body parts. If sliced in half, the head end will grow a new tail and the tail end will grow a new head! Some species of these tiny flat worms are also good as mosquito predators. Planarians glide along the underside of the surface film. They catch and eat mosquito larva and pupae as they come to the surface to breath. The mosquitoes are trapped in mucus produced by the slow-moving flatworms. Planarians will even eat egg rafts!

Can planaria be used to help control mosquitoes in urban environments? Researchers have been studying planaria to determine their potential as mosquito control agents. Brown planaria, *Dugesia dorotocephala,* have proven to be the best predator among the many species tested in laboratory conditions. These planaria have shown to be resistant to the chemicals commonly used to control mosquitoes. They are easy to store and can survive long periods of time without food. Thus they lend themselves to being shipped to sites where they will be used. However, this is another example of releasing a potentially foreign organism into another ecosystem.

Several predaceous **invertebrates** and plants have been tested and used as urban mosquito control agents. **Diving beetle larvae, backswimmers**, certain copepods, and hydras have proven to be good mosquito larvae predators. Some plants such as bladderworts prey on mosquito larvae. They catch them in their "bladders" when a larva or other prey organism swims into the plant, tripping a small trigger that activates the bladder, causing it to rapidly expand and suck in the prey item. The prey is then broken down within the bladder by digestive enzymes produced by the plant.

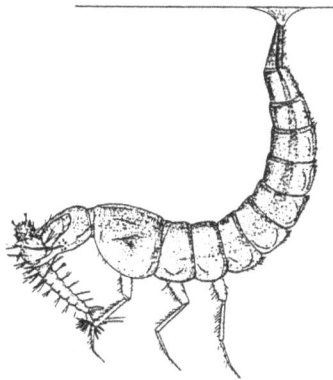

Dytisid adult beetle

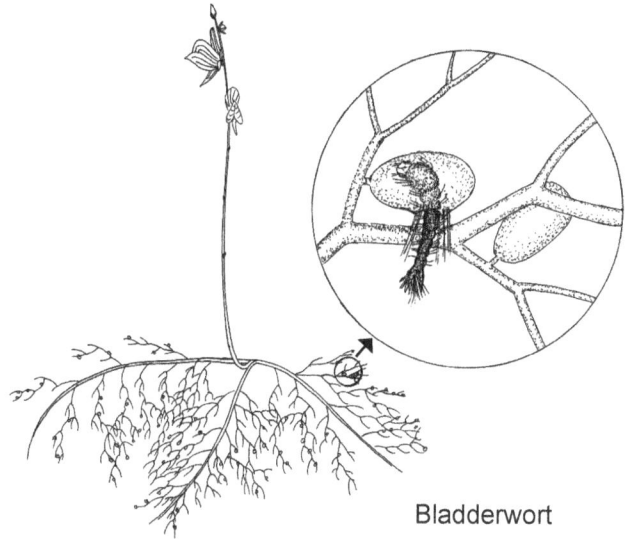

Dytisid larva eating mosquito larva

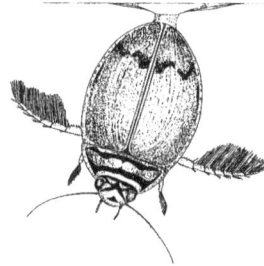

Bladderwort

The cannibal mosquitoes, genus *Toxorhynchites* or "Tox" mosquitoes, are reared and released by some mosquito control agencies. They are very useful in controlling mosquitoes that breed in artificial containers, such as yellow fever mosquitoes and Asian tiger mosquitoes. The larvae of these large, metallic coloured mosquitoes are "cannibals", feeding on other kinds of mosquito larvae. Adult Tox mosquitoes only feed on plant juices. They cause no harm to people or domestic animals.

Adult Tox mosquitoes are released at dusk. This keeps these slow-flying mosquitoes from being eaten by birds before they can lay their eggs. Females search for tree holes and artificial containers holding water and other mosquito larvae. The female will hover near a water container as she flicks the tip of her abdomen, tossing large white eggs into the water.

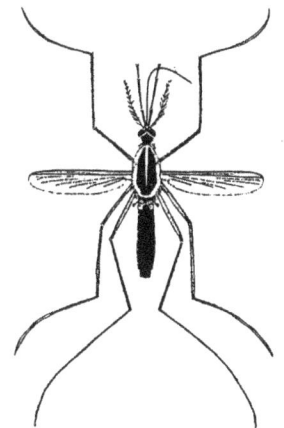

Tox adult

Soon after hatching, the brown to rust-coloured Tox larvae begin to feed. As they get older, they begin to catch other mosquito larvae with their special grasping mouthparts. A Tox larva consumes many mosquitoes before it develops into an adult.

Tax larvae

Used under the right conditions, Tox mosquitoes are good mosquito control agents. The females can find hidden breeding sites that survey technicians may miss. The larvae are good predators, quickly reducing numbers of pest mosquitoes growing in artificial containers. They can also survive long periods without food. Tox larvae cannot control mosquitoes by themselves, but used correctly they can play a valuable contributing role in urban mosquito control, reducing the amount of insecticides used.

Several birds are effective predators of adult mosquitoes. Many species of birds (flycatchers, martins, swallows, warblers and others) consume many mosquitoes by capturing their prey as they fly. When the mosquitoes hatch during the rainy season, Belize has added numbers of the mosquito-eating bird species migrating from North America. Some bat species are good mosquito predators, being active during the time when many blood-feeding mosquitoes are also active.

dragon fly

Dragonflies can also reduce mosquito numbers significantly, especially when these fast-flying and agile predators occur in large numbers. Other predetors include geckos and anoles.

Purple Martins

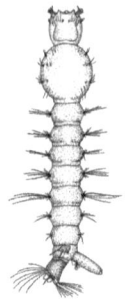

Reducing Mosquito Breeding Habitats

Container-breeding mosquitoes pose a special problem in many towns. An old tire or bucket tossed in the weeds can produce mosquitoes for years. Even a bottle or jar will breed hundreds of mosquitoes. Mosquitoes breed in clogged rain gutters, water vats, animal watering bowls and troughs, flower pots, and coconut shells, just to list a few sites. Imagine how many water-holding containers are scattered throughout a village, town or city!

The best way to control container-breeding mosquitoes is to remove the containers. Clean out rain gutters and watering troughs. Screen rainwater vats. Clean up litter along roadsides and from vacant lots, removing old tires, getting rid of broken down washing machines and other backyard clutter. A great many mosquitoes can be removed with a single, community-supported spring clean-up day. A successful clean-up day will reduce the amount of pesticides used to control mosquitoes and beautify the neighbourhood.

In the early days of mosquito control, one strategy used was to drain swamps and marshes to reduce breeding sites. However, swamps and marshes are critical wetland habitats that perform many important ecological services. We need to protect our wetlands and even restore them where possible. Mosquito control in these ecosystems is best achieved with naturally occurring predators. Even though nuisance mosquitoes can emerge from wetland areas, urban breeding sites produce many species that are vectors of human pathogens and parasites.

Urban drainage ditches, especially those contaminated by sewage, or clogged with sediment and debris, can be an important source of southern house mosquitoes and other species. Opening up drainage ditches and getting stagnant water to flow will help to reduce mosquitoes. Also, routine treatment with Bth-14, spraying these sites once a week, can be an effective solution. In addition, addressing the causes of sewage contamination is important, reducing the nutrients entering these streams, which both eliminates the input of human pathogens into surface water and improves effectiveness of Bth-14 if it is being applied. If ditches hold water permanently, ensuring the presence of local mosquito-eating fishes may be an effective control method.

Often the occurrence of *Anopheles darlingi,* a very effective malaria vector, is increased if debris and garbage discarded into larger streams and rivers is captured and held, building up as floating detritus mats in back pools. This increases the amount of breeding sites, therefore increasing mosquitoe populations. Discouraging people from clearing **riparian** vegetation and tossing cut material into streams and rivers, or disposing of garbage into these systems can help keep available habitats to a minimum.

It is important to remember that permanent mosquito habitats are generally inhabited by many other organisms, some of those being very important predators of mosquitoes or may be providing key environmental services. Any control method we implement should not impose negative effects on these other organisms of the ecosystem.

Personal Protection from Mosquitoes

There are many things that we can all do to protect ourselves and our families from biting mosquitoes. Wearing long sleeve, light-coloured shirts and long pants when outside at dusk is a good way to reduce mosquito bites. There are many kinds of mosquito repellents on the store shelves today. Many of these have "DEET" and other chemicals in them that have proven to effectively repel mosquitoes. Repellents come in many formulations, such as lotions, creams, waxy sticks, and sprays. They also come in several different strengths. Citronella and other botanical oils are also been used as a mosquito repellents, providing alternatives to DEET-based repellents.

Mosquito biting activity usually tends to increase significantly for a couple of hours just after sunset. Planning indoor activities during this time can help reduce exposure. If you or your family have outdoor activities planned during this time, wearing appropriate clothing and perhaps using a repellent is advisable.

Some mosquito species slip into our houses and bite us at night while we are sleeping. We can protect ourselves by keeping window screens in good repair. Widespread use of window screening is probably the single most important factor in eradicating malaria from the southern United States. In areas where mosquitoes cannot be easily screened out of the house, sleep under a **mosquito net**. Be sure to hang the netting so that it will not tear easily. Tuck the edges in around the mattress at night. Repair any small holes you find in your netting. It is particularly important for those persons suffering from malaria, dengue fever, chikungunya, and Zika to sleep under mosquito nets when they are in the infective stage. This will prevent spreading these diseases to other people by preventing mosquitoes from becoming infected.

Getting to Know Your Mosquito Control Agency

Some towns and cities have a mosquito control programme. Programmes may involve just spraying chemicals around town to kill adult mosquitoes. They may only have one truck with a spray machine mounted on the back. The truck may only run a couple of hours once every week or two. In other countries mosquito control programmes may operate fleets of trucks. A few large metropolitan programmes around the world have their own airplanes and helicopters for aerial spraying. They may have larvicide crews, surveillance teams, and public relations people. Some of these larger programmes also conduct disease surveillance and test new control agents and equipment. Many control programmes work with local universities on mosquito research projects. A few programmes rear biological control agents.

In Belize, the **Ministry of Health's Vector Control Programme** is concerned with mosquito control activities. Technicians become involved in survey efforts to assess problems and help develop effective control strategies, particularly for those mosquito species that carry diseases. Professionals within this programme are a good source of information concerning mosquito issues and effective control strategies. Find out what kinds of mosquito control activities are going on in your community or nearby towns.

Involving Your Community

We are all responsible for helping to prevent excessive mosquito breeding within our villages, towns, and cities. Sometimes we get very busy with our work or school. We forget to do our part to help make our community safe and enjoyable for both ourselves and others. A nice reminder is sometimes needed to jog our memories.

Many people throughout towns and cities grow mosquitoes in their backyards. Perhaps they have just gotten a little careless. They forgot to turn over the washtub or boat. Maybe they just haven't gotten round to hauling off that old washing machine. Maybe they have let a few old tires stack up behind the garage. Many people do not know that mosquitoes breed in water.

You can help. Come up with ways to remind your community what they can do to help reduce mosquito numbers. Remind them of the importance of mosquitoes as disease vectors. Together we can help control mosquito populations. Your school or active community group can make a big contribution by organizing a local clean-up effort. Working with your local government officials, schools, and community organizations, many breeding sites can be removed to reduce the problem. You can also report illegal dumping of garbage and discourage such activities in your area.

Community support and participation is vital to the success of urban mosquito control programmes. Working together we can create a cleaner, safer and more healthy environment for everyone.

Conclusion

Mosquitoes are very important in the lives of many people around the world. However, as a community we often know very little about them, where they breed, how they behave, the diseases they can carry, and actions we can take to reduce their numbers around our homes. Often we help to rear the very mosquitoes that cause most of our problems. Hopefully *The Mosquito Book* has served to introduce people, particularly youth, to the science of mosquito biology, ecology and population management by addressing such topics as:

- the intricate life cycle of mosquito species that affect our health and well-being;

- other organisms that share aquatic habitats with mosquitoes;

- ecological requirements of mosquitoes for growth, development and reproduction;

- roles humans play in the life cycles of many mosquitoes;

- issues involving the exclusive use of chemicals for mosquito control;

- alternative non-chemical mosquito control techniques; and

- the importance of community involvement and education for realizing success in an effective mosquito control programme.

Glossary

Because some specific words used in scientific writing come from the Latin, grammatical Latin patterns are used. For example, the plural of nouns ending in "a" is "ae". The singular word is used in this glossary, but plural (pl) and adjectival (adj) forms are also given.

abdomen, abdominal (adj)—within the insects this is the body segment that is behind the thorax, the posterior of the body.

adulticiding—strategies for killing adult biting insects, often by spraying chemical insecticides.

antenna, antennae (pl)—a pair of segmented, movable sensory appendages on the heads of insects.

arrow plants—emergent aquatic or wetland plants in the genus *Sagittaria* that have arrow-shaped leaves, their bases often serving as habitat area for mosquito larvae, affording them some protection from predators.

artificial containers—human-made containers such as discarded tires, metal cans, glass jars, old washing machines and anything else that holds water provides breeding sites for mosquitoes.

artificial container breeders—those mosquitoes that tend to use or exclusively use artificial containers as breeding sites.

backswimmers—aquatic true bugs (order *Hemiptera*) that belong to the family *Notonectidae* and typically swim on their backs, ventral surface facing upwards.

bacterium, bacteria (pl)—a single-celled organism having chromosomes suspended in the cytoplasm of a cell rather than bound up within a nuclear membrane.

biofilm—a living film that grows on surfaces (rock, sediment, wood, shells, skin of living organism, plastic, metal, etc) that are submerged in water or kept moist, consisting of bacteria and their secretions, microscopic fungi, diatoms, algae, protozoa, and microscopic invertebrates; an important food source for many aquatic organisms, such as many aquatic insects.

biological control—use of natural predators, pathogens and parasites that prey on or infect mosquitoes that can be used to control mosquito populations.

bladderworts—small floating aquatic plants in the genus *Utricularia* that have tiny bladders attached to their roots that can capture small aquatic insects such as mosquito larvae that the plant uses as a source of nitrogen.

breathing tube—a structure on tip of the abdomen of many mosquito larvae or on the head of mosquito pupae that can attach to the surface film and allow larvae and mosquitoes to breath air.

Bth-14—an abbreviation for *Bacillus thuringiensus israelensis*, a commercially available bacterial spore in several formulations (powder, liquid, granular) used by many mosquito control agencies as an effective and target-specific larvicide, not affecting most other aquatic organisms.

bulrush—wetland plants in the family *Juncaceae* with round, hollow stems that may have partitions inside, often forming habitats along shorelines used by mosquito larvae.

cannibal mosquitoes—large mosquitoes in the genus *Toxorhynchites* whose larvae feed on other species of mosquito larvae but the adults do not feed on blood, sometimes raised and released in urban areas for biological mosquito control.

capillaries—the smallest blood vessels that connect the arteries and veins together, the blood vessels from which mosquitoes and other blood-sucking arthropods typically feed.

carbon dioxide—the gas that is exhaled by respiring organisms, and that attracts adult female mosquitoes that can follow the carbon dioxide trail to a potential blood meal.

cattails—tall reedy wetland plants in the genus *Typha* that put on long fruiting spikes, their thick growth along pond and river edges creating habitat for mosquito larvae that are protected from many predators.

chikungunya—a virus-induced disease transmitted from the reservoir host (monkeys, cattle, rodents, birds) to person and from person to person by the bite of *Aedes agypti* or *A. albopictus*.

cocoon—a silk case that some insect larvae spin around themselves for protection while they undergo metamorphosis during the pupae phase of their life cycle.

community—a group of different species of microbes, plants, animals, and fungi that live together and interact within a particular habitat.

copepods—small, often tear-drop-shaped, aquatic crustaceans that live within many mosquito breeding habitats, some species of copepods being predaceous on mosquito larvae.

DEET—diethyltoluamide, an organic compound that is put in most insect repellents.

dengue fever—an acute infection caused by a virus carried by *Aedes* mosquitoes (especially *Aedes agypti* and *A albopictus*) that shows symptoms of headaches, rashes, and severe pain in the joints, also called "breakbone fever".

dengue haemorrhagic fever—a life-threatening complication of dengue fever with bleeding, reduced blood platelets and extremely blood pressure.

detritus—dead plant material found in soil and water that is decomposed by fungi and bacteria within biofilm communities as a food source.

diatom—single-celled photosynthetic organism that secretes a silica dioxide or glass case around itself; occurs in fresh and salt water, living as plankton or attached to underwater surfaces on stalks, and serves as food for many different kinds of small animals.

diving beetle—predatory aquatic beetles in the family *Dytiscidae* that will feed on mosquito larvae, diving beetle larvae breathing underwater by gills and adults breathing underwater from air bubbles trapped under their outer wings.

dog heartworms—mosquito-transmitted worms (*Dirofilaria immitis*) that infect dogs, with adult worms amassing in heart and ultimately preventing the heart from functioning properly.

ecology—a life science that focuses on the study of the interrelationships among organisms and their environments, all the patterns of relationships among organisms and their environments (including rocks, soil, water, air, and other living forms).

egg rafts—clusters of eggs laid by mosquitoes in the genus *Culex* that are glued together into little floating rafts that sit upon the surface film of still water bodies.

elephantiasis—a disease that involves the enlargement of limbs and scrotum caused by mosquito-transmitted worms (*Wuchereria bancrofti*) that block the lymphatic system, causing excessive accumulation of fluid in the tissue.

encephalitis—inflammation of the brain and brain stem tissue, often caused by virus infection, many of those viruses being carried by mosquitoes or other vectors.

entomologist—a biologist who specializes in studying insects or select groups of insects.

epidemic—the outbreak of an infectious disease that affects a large number of people or other organisms by the causative agent (pathogen, parasite).

exuvia—the molted outer skeleton or chiton skin of an insect.

float hairs—tiny hydrophobic or water repelling hairs that line the opening of the breathing siphon of a mosquito larva, acting to both prevent water from entering the siphon, and serving as an anchor that attaches to larva to the surface film and allows it to hang there without having to use energy to swim.

floodwater mosquitoes—a group of mosquitoes that typically lay their eggs in soil within depressions or just above the water level of pools and ponds so that soil and eggs are flooded by rising water levels during heavy rainy periods, with larvae hatching and growing rapidly.

fungus, fungi (pl)—a kingdom of spore-producing organisms that produce the enzyme cellulase that can digest dead plant material (leaves, wood), or are sometimes parasites on living organisms; very important in breaking down dead plant material in aquatic systems and are a major food source for other organisms.

genus—a category of biological identification that ranks between the family and the species, encompassing a group of species within a family that share a unique characteristic setting them apart from other species within that family; when a genus name is written, whether alone or with a species name attached, it is capitalized and either underlined if hand-written or printed in italics: *Aedes*, or *Aedes agypti*.

habitat—the area within an ecosystem in which a specific species of plant or animal lives.

halteres—a pair of club-shaped structures on true flies in the order *Diptera* that serve as sensors and flight stabilizers; they are formed in place of the second pair of wings.

host—the living plant or animal in or on which a parasite lives.

hydra—small primitive freshwater animals in the phylum *Coelenerata* that have tentacles equipped with stinging cells for capturing small organisms for food, including mosquito larvae.

instar—that stage within the life cycle of an arthropod occurring between any two successive molts.

integrated mosquito control—the use of many different strategies, including chemicals, biological control agents, reduction of breeding sites, public awareness, and surveys to control mosquito populations within an area.

invertebrates—animals that lack a spinal column, which includes most of the species within the animal kingdom.

larva, larvae (pl)—the feeding and growing stage within the life cycle of an insect that goes through complete metamorphosis; the stage between the egg and the pupa.

larviciding—use of chemicals or biological control agents to kill mosquito larvae within aquatic habitats.

lymph system—part of the body's circulatory system that collects fluids and proteins that have leaked from cells and tissues and transports this material to the blood.

malaria—an old disease caused by a sporozoan parasite in the genus *Plasmodium*, transmitted from human to human by the bite of *Anopheles*, that invades and destroys the red blood cells, symptoms often being periodic attacks of chills and fever.

malathion—an organo-phosphate pesticide used to control a wide range of insects, including mosquitoes, that is less acutely toxic to mammals than other pesticides within this class.

metamorphosis—a very obvious physical change that occurs in many animals when they are leaving one growth phase and entering another, as when a mosquito pupa transforms to an adult mosquito.

microcephaly—a serious birth defect that results in babies with very small heads and under-developed brains.

micro-droplets—very tiny droplets of insecticide dispersed from ultra-low volume insecticide applicators that allow the chemical to stay suspended in the air longer, drift further, and spread over a larger area, potentially contacting more target insects.

molt—the shedding of the skin or exoskeleton of an arthropod so that its body can expand in size and a new exoskeleton can grow larger and then harden.

mosquito fish—a group of small fishes in the genus *Gambusia* that bear live young rather than lay eggs, and that specialize in feeding on organisms at the surface of the water, including mosquito larvae.

mosquito net—a fine mesh net that fits over a bed to protect a person from biting mosquitoes at night while he or she is sleeping.

mouth brushes—stiff hairs surrounding the mouth of mosquito larvae that help filter out small organic particles from the water, coated with bacteria that are used as food by the larvae.

muck buckets—a bucket or other container that has purposefully had a little cow manure, wet rotting leaves or other decomposing organic material added to make it more attractive to mosquitoes ready to lay eggs.

nematodes—long, cylindrical worms, also called "roundworms", that are found living in soil and water or as parasites in many other organisms, several species being human parasites carried from human to human by the bite of certain species of mosquitoes.

ovitraps—plastic jars or cans filled with water up to an overflow hole punched in the side, with a wooden paddle or strip of sandpaper stuck in the water attached to the inside of the jar, providing a rough surface for a container breeding mosquito to lay eggs above the water line, used as a survey tool to determine the presence of *Aedes aegypti* mosquitoes in an area.

palpus, palpi (pl)—a segmented projection of an arthropod mouthpart; projections on either side of a mosquito proboscis, being almost as long as the proboscis in *Anopheles* mosquitos and short in other common mosquito genera.

parasites—organisms that live on or inside of other organisms (hosts) from which they draw subsistence or benefits while causing harm to its host.

pathogens—specific organisms, such as bacteria, that infest other organisms, creating disease symptoms in their hosts.

permanent water mosquitoes—those mosquito species whose larvae are predominately associated with permanent water bodies such as ponds, lakes, and rivers.

pesticide applicators—people who have been trained to handle and responsibly apply pesticides while using prescribed health precautions.

pesticides—chemical compounds that have been designed and manufactured to kill certain kinds of organisms identified as pests, such as mosquitoes, flies, roaches (insecticides), nematodes (nematocides), weeds (herbicides), and fungi (fungicides).

pitcher plants—plants in the family *Sarraceniaceae* with leaves modified into containers that hold water in which insects become trapped and digested by enzymes secreted by the pitcher plants; the larvae of some mosquito species can live and survive within these aquatic habitats created by pitcher plants.

planarians—small, grey or dark-coloured freshwater flatworms in the family *Planariidae* that have two eye spots, triangular-shaped heads, and a well-developed ability to regenerate lost parts and become whole worms if cut into pieces; sometimes effective predators of mosquito larvae when they are attached to the surface film.

predators—animals that prey on other animals, eating them as a primary food source.

proboscis—the elongated tubular mouthpart of an adult mosquito used to inject into capillaries and suck blood from a host.

protozoan, protozoa (pl)—single-celled organisms that make up the kingdom *Protista*, and include flagellates, amoebas, and ciliates, each of which represents a phylum within *Protista*; several species of protozoa cause diseases in humans and are transmitted from host to host by mosquitoes and other blood-feeding insects.

pupa, pupae (pl)—the non-feeding stage within the life cycle of an insect that goes through complete metamorphosis; the stage between the larva and the adult during which metamorphosis takes place.

resistance—after long-term exposure, sometimes specific pesticides are no longer effective at controlling the target pest population; many mosquito populations have developed resistance to malathion.

roundworm—common name for nematodes, many species of nematodes being parasites on many different kinds of organisms, including humans.

scientific name—the unique genus and species name that is assigned to every species of living organism that has been described within the scientific literature. For example, *Culex quinquefaciatus* is the name given to the southern house mosquito, where "*Culex*" is the genus name and "*quinquefaciatus*" is the species name; a name that is accepted around the world among scientists and administrators, because many species have many different common names in different places in the world, and sometimes within the same region.

segment—refers to the body parts of arthropods, each part (head, thorax, abdomen) representing groups of body pieces that have fused together. For example, the pair of appendages for each segment evolved specialized functions: head-antennae, each set of mouth parts, thorax-wings, and legs.

seta, setae (pl)—a slender, usually stiff and springy bristle extending from the dermal surface, legs, and/or mouth parts of an insect or other organism.

siphon—a tubular structure of an animal's body that is used to draw in or expel air or water; a mosquito larva often has a siphon for air exchange on the end of its abdomen and a mosquito pupa has two siphons for breathing air, one attached to either side of its head.

species—a category of classification for organisms that is below genus or sub-genus and encompasses those populations of organisms capable of interbreeding and producing viable offspring; the second name designated in a scientific name, as in *Anopheles darling*, "*darling*" being the species name, written in lower case following the capitalized genus name.

sporozoite—motile and infectious stage of some sporozoan parasites, such as *Plasmodium vivax* and *P falciparium* that cause malaria in humans.

springtails—small, primitive, wingless insects in the order *Collembola* that use a structure called a "furcula" that operates like a spring-powered lever to propel the insect forward; often found on the surface tension layer within mosquito-breeding habitats.

surface tension—the molecule-thick film of hydrogen-bonded water molecules stretched over the surface of a water body, a film so strong that many kinds of insects can suspend from it, walk across it, or become stuck to it.

survey—a rapid visual assessment of a landscape or area and/or interview of community members to identify natural features of interest, such as wetlands, temporary pools, ponds, lakes, streams and rivers; human-built structures, activities, and impacts, such as buildings, waste piles, water tanks, cleared land, pastures; and, in this case, water bodies that are positive for mosquito larvae; all recorded, mapped, and described for use as a planning and action tool.

taxonomic key—a document or book that assists in the identification of an organism by describing body structure and characteristics, usually within numbered alternate pairs of descriptive statements supported with illustrations or photographs, with the statement that best describes the organism in question referencing the next set of numbered alternate pairs of statements, and so forth, until a name is arrived at (family, genus, and species) in the final pair.

taxonomists—scientists who specialize in identifying, describing, and cataloguing new families, genera, and species within particular groups of organisms.

thermofogger—a spray machine, often mounted on the back of a pickup truck, where a mixture of pesticide and diesel is sprayed onto a hot manifold to produce a thick white fog that spreads through the air.

thorax—the segment of an insect's body between the head and the abdomen; the segment to which legs and wings are attached.

tire recappers—people and companies that add new rubber tread to old tire cores to produce recapped tires.

tox mosquitoes—large mosquitoes in the genus *Toxorhynchites* whose larvae prey on mosquito species and are sometimes used as biological control agents for other human biting mosquito species.

tumblers—a common name for the pupae stage of mosquitoes, so named because of their tumbling swimming behaviour.

vectors—animals that carry disease agents that they transmit from one host to another; mechanical vectors pick up disease causing agents when walking over faeces and rotting organic material, dispersing them when the vector then walks across food and eating utensils; biological vectors harbour the disease-causing agents in their bodies where the disease organisms undergo part of their life cycle before being introduced to the next host.

virus—very simple sub-microscopic organism or complex organic molecules (still in debate) made up of a protein shell surrounding nucelic acid that can only grow and reproduce within living cells of other organisms; many viruses cause serious diseases in humans and some are transmitted from human to human by mosquitoes.

water striders—long-legged true insects of the family *Gerridae* that can move around on the surface tension of a water body.

wetland—land areas, marshes, and swamps that are periodically, seasonally inundated by shallow water and/or soils are saturated with water.

yellow fever—an acute disease found in tropical and sub-tropical areas characterized by loss of energy, fever, headaches, and sometimes jaundice and bleeding; caused by a *Flavivirus* that is transmitted from person to person by mosquitoes in the genus *Aedes.*

Zika—a virus carried by infected mosquitoes *(Aedes aegypti* and *Aedes albopictus)* causing headaches, rash, fever, conjunctivitis (red eyes), joint pains, and microcephaly, a birth defect resulting in babies with very small heads and under-developed brains.

References

Benenson, A. S. (ed.), 1985. *Control of Communicable Diseases in Man*. 14th Edition. Washington DC: The American Public Health Association.

Bertram, D. S. 1971. Mosquitoes of British Honduras, with Some Comments on Malaria, and on Arbovirus Antibodies in Man and Equines. *Transactions of the Royal Society of Tropical Medicine and Hygiene*. 65(2): 742- 762.

Bruce-Chwatt, L.J., 1985. *Essential Malariology*. 2nd Edition. New York NY: John Wiley and Sons.

Carpenter, S.J. & LaCasse, W.J., 1955. *Mosquitoes of North America (North Mexico)*. Berkley CA: University of California Press.

Carroll, L. and S. Sarmiento, 2016. 'Striking' Results from Early Zika Vaccine Trial. *NBCNews* <www.nbcnews.com/storyline/zika-virus-outbreak/striking-results-early-zika-vaccine-trial-n623016>.

Ebering, W., 1978. Urban Entomology. *Division of Agricultural Sciences*. Berkley CA: University of California Press.

Fassett, N.C., 1940. *A Manual of Aquatic Plants*. New York NY: McGraw-Hill Book Company, Inc.

Foote, R.H. & Cook, D.R., 1959. Mosquitoes of Medical Importance. *Agriculture Handbook* No. 152, Agricultural Research Service, Washington DC: U.S. Department of Agriculture.

Furman, D.P. & Catts, E.P., 1982. *Manual of Entomology*. 4th Edition. Cambridge: Cambridge University Press.

Gillett, J.D., 1972. *The Mosquito: Its life, Activities and Impact on Human Affairs*. Garden City New York: Doubleday and Company, Inc.

Global Health Group Country Briefing, 2012. *Eliminating Malaria in Belize*. <globalhealthsciences.ucsf.edu/sites/default/files/content/ghg/country-briefings/Belize.pdf>.

Horsfall, W.R., 1962. *Medical Entomology; Arthropods and Human Disease*. New York NY: The Ronald Press Company.

James, M.T. & Harwood, R.F., 1979. *Entomology in Human and Animal Health*. 7th Edition. New York NY: MacMillan Publishing Company, Inc.

Lounibos, L.P., Rey, J.R. & Frank, J.H. (eds), 1985. *Ecology of Mosquitoes: Proceedings of a Workshop*. Vero Beach FL: Florida Medical Entomology Laboratory.

Meek, C.L. & Hayes, C.R. (eds), 1984. *Commercial Pesticide Applicator Mosquito Control Training Manual*. Louisiana Mosquito Control Association.

Merritt, R.W. & K.W. Cummins, (eds), 1996. *An Introduction to The Aquatic Insects of North America*. Dubuque IO: Kendall/Hunt Publishing Company.

Pecor, J. E., R. E. Harbach, E. L. Peyton, D. R. Roberts, E. Rejmankova, S. Manguin, and J. Palanko. 2002. Mosquito studies in Belize, Central America: Records, Taxonomic Notes, and Checklist of Species. *Journal of the American Mosquito Control Association* 18(4): 241-276.

Pennak, R.W. 1953. *Fresh-water Invertebrates of The United States*. New York NY: The Roland Press Company.

San Pedro Sun, 2015. *2015 Already Registering Record Number of Dengue Outbreaks* <sanpedrosun.com/health/2015/08/13/2015-already-registering-record-number-dengue-outbreaks>.

Steele, J.H. (editor-in-chief) 1982. *CRC Handbook Series in Zoonoses*. Volumes I, II & III. Boca Raton, FL: CRC Press, Inc.

U.S. Department of Health and Human Services. 1987. *Self Study Course 3013-g Vector-Borne Disease Control: Mosquitoes*. Atlanta GA: Center for Disease Control Training and Laboratory Program.

www.ingramcontent.com/pod-product-compliance
Lightning Source LLC
Chambersburg PA
CBHW041426270326
41931CB00023B/3492